Eastern Counties
Edited by Heather Killingray

First published in Great Britain in 2006 by:
Young Writers
Remus House
Coltsfoot Drive
Peterborough
PE2 9JX
Telephone: 01733 890066
Website: www.youngwriters.co.uk

All Rights Reserved

© Copyright Contributors 2006

SB ISBN 1 84602 382 3

Foreword

This year, the Young Writers' *POP! - The Power Of Poetry* competition proudly presents a showcase of the best poetic talent selected from thousands of up-and-coming writers nationwide.

Young Writers was established in 1991 to promote the reading and writing of poetry within schools and to the young of today. Our books nurture and inspire confidence in the ability of young writers and provide a snapshot of poems written in schools and at home by budding poets of the future.

The thought, effort, imagination and hard work put into each poem impressed us all and the task of selecting poems was a difficult but nevertheless enjoyable experience.

We hope you are as pleased as we are with the final selection and that you and your family continue to be entertained with *POP! Eastern Counties* for many years to come.

Contents

Attleborough High School, Attleborough

James Thacker (13)	1
Philip Starling (15)	1
Elisabeth Rickard (15)	2
Paige Perfect (14)	2
Nicholas Colchester (14)	3
Sarah Newby (14)	3
Amy Montgomerie (14)	4
Laura Holland (14)	4
Emma Dean (15)	5
James Baldwin (14)	5
Elanor Hall (14)	6
Sian Duval (15)	7
Amber Bradbury (14)	8
Rachael Dickenson (15)	8
Heather Briggs (14)	9
Hannah Chenery (12)	9
Sean Craemer (16)	9
Evelyn Edwards (12)	10
Jennifer Davey (14)	11
Hannah Clifford (14)	12
Sam Bodmer (14)	12
Emily Follows (12)	13
Jack Lebbell (12)	13
Benjamin Brown (12)	13
Thomas King-Fisher (15)	14
Daniel Forde (12)	14
Sophie Barker (13)	15
Kenneth Williams (12)	15
Kerri Morgan (16)	16
Sam Pickles (14)	16
Tom Bulmer (12)	17
Matthew Rogers (11)	17
Natasha Doyle (16)	18
Ashley Gowland (12)	18
Alicia Lacey (12)	19
Beth Reeve (11)	19
Rachel Fleming (11)	20
Luke Downs (13)	20

Sofia Dodson (12)	20
Michael Edghill (11)	21
Charlie Joe Burnage (11)	21
Kayleigh Briggs (14)	22
Charlotte Willis (11)	22
Dominic Hazell (11)	23
Savanna Kmecik (13)	23
Joe Smith (12)	23
Joanna Slater (11)	24
Matthew Freeman (11)	24
Georgia Whyman (11)	24
Luke Hughes (11)	25
Thomas Curtis (11)	25
Adam Turner (12)	25
Lorna Allen (12)	26
Jasmine Card (11)	26
Thomas Saunders (12)	27
Sophie McKenna (11)	27
Michaela Fiddy (12)	28
Sophie Binks (12)	28
Victoria Moore (12)	29
Tyne Courtney & Bri Murray (12)	30
Christina Martell (12)	30
Jacob Peckett (12)	31
Rebecca Etteridge (12)	31
Victoria Watling (12)	32
Kerry Cross (12)	32
Hollie Judge (13)	32
Anna Blaser (12)	33
Bethany Gibbs (12)	33
Josh Whiterod (12)	34
Jason Sturman (12)	34
Kathryn Mather (13)	34
Joshua Bunn (12)	35
Ashley Davis (12)	35
Molly Naldrett (12)	36
Ciaron Amos (14)	36
Amy Horth (12)	36
Josie Pinnock (13)	37
Alice Fletcher (13)	37
Chris Cromack (13)	38
Ciaran Long (12)	38

Josh Downes (12)	38
Jason Miller (13)	39
Luke Mitchell (13)	39
Kirsty Clarke (13)	39
Kim Wild (14)	40
Robert Warren (13)	40
Shaun Banham (12)	41
Andrew Johnson (13)	41
Danny Moore (12)	42
Sean Robinson (13)	42
Rosie Waugh (13)	42
Laura Gipp (13)	43
Lauren Rapley (13)	43
Hannah Goward (11)	43
Norman Stillwell (16)	44
Hermione Howson (13)	44
Elliott Heading (17)	45
Emily Broad (13)	45
Jessica Sacharczuk (13)	46
Ryan Saunders (13)	46
Gemma Snelling (13)	46
Carla Moore (11)	47
Philip Mickleborough (11)	47
Mark Anderson-Wilson (13)	47
Sarah Pickersgill (16)	48
Ryan Moore (13)	49
Katherine Humphreys (11)	49
Toby Clements (11)	50
Louis Gyde (13)	50
Abby Richards (11)	51
Sam Lawrence (13)	51
Chloe Babel (11)	52
Persia Winter (11)	52
Serena Suggitt (11)	52
Connie Holliday (11)	53
Hannah Carr (12)	53
Jamie Potts (11)	53
Danny White (11)	54
Jamie Henderson (11)	54
Edward Tyce (11)	54
Chris Merry (11)	55
Taila Hunt (11)	55

Keeley Hoyte (11) 55
Jack Skipper 56
Emma Seville (11) 56
Tiffany Bolingbroke (11) 57
Polly Fyson (11) 57
George Harrison (11) 57
Demi Long (11) 58

Braeside Senior School, Buckhurst Hill
Georgina Pipe (13) 58
Vanessa Hoh (12) 58
Sanya Akhtar (12) 58
Helen Walker (12) 59
Shana Patel (12) 59
Lydia Smith (12) 59
Lucy Benham Whyte (12) 59
Iesha Agyemang (12) 60
Gabrielle Compton (12) 60
Samantha Staab (12) 60
Emily Benham Whyte (12) 60
Rebecca Bushell (13) 61
Isabelle Docker (13) 61
Alexandria Martin (13) 61
Rebecca Lee (13) 62
Nicole Abbott (13) 62
Holly Chapman (12) 62
Skye Jacobs (14) 63
Natalie Stone (13) 63
Sophie Goodhew (13) 64
Chloe O'Connor (13) 64
Sitara Ali (12) 64
Christiana Bourne (13) 65
Francesca Higgins (13) 65
Alexandra Jack (13) 65
Jenna Brown (13) 66
Shehana Udat (13) 67
Lucy Brunt (13) 68

Bury St Edmunds County Upper School, Bury St Edmunds
Toni Gidney (13) 68
Ashley Bugg (13) 69

Alex Henshaw (13)	69
Ryan Bailey (13)	69
Kersha Haynes (13)	70
James Scott (13)	70
Sophie Nichols (13)	70
Jo Jones (13)	71
Sarah Button (13)	71
Adam Redfern (13)	72
Rebecca Guy (13)	72
Laura Anders (14)	73
Samantha Ashford (13)	73
Bethany Raper (13)	74
Sammy Boscheck (15)	74
Adam Farrant (14)	74
Emily Ruddock (13)	75
Hattie Wright (13)	75
Tatiana Golden-Collinson (13)	76
Ashley Hardy (13)	76
Beth Newton (13)	77
Jordan Wiemer (13)	77
Josh Foster Brown (13)	78
Élodie Limer (13)	79
Millie Packer (14)	80
Jack Kimber (13)	80
Keiran Wingfield (14)	81
Daniel Kemp (13)	81
Simon Johns (14)	82
Rachel Cox (13)	82
Alicia Hardy (14)	83
Meg Shorten (13)	83
Gemma Candy (14)	84
Juliet Mills (13)	84
Aiden Hughes (13)	85
Scarlett Brabrook (13)	85
Emily Victoria Webb (13)	86
Ollie Clements (13)	86
Amber Warren & Emma Cochrane (13)	87
Kim Lumbis (14)	87
Katie Mathers (14)	88
Sam Welham (13)	88
Josh Turner (13)	89
Harley Miller (13)	89

Amy Manning (13)	89
Andrew Kimpton (13)	90
Rob Plumb (13)	90
Jonathan Moffat (13)	90
Lauren Harker (13)	91
Emily Cawston (13)	91
Gemma Manning (13)	92
Jack Brame (13)	92
Hannah Otterson (13)	92
Lana Watson (13)	93

Fulbrook Middle School, Woburn Sands

Matthew Greenwell (10)	93
Georgia Pulford (10)	94
Timothy Byrne (10)	94

Greensward College, Hockley

Dan Cause (16)	95
Greg Longman (12)	95
Emily Higgs & Chloe Graham (12)	96
Katey Horrocks (13)	96
Katie Chamberlain (12)	97
James Hull (15)	97
David Edgington (12)	97
Stephanie Hawkes (12)	98
Sophie Hand (12)	98
Hannah Brookes (12)	99
Katie Robinson (12)	99
Georgia Branton (12)	100
Sarah Williams (12)	100
Toby Challis (12)	101
Paul Hixson (12)	101
Olivia Kinsman (12)	102
Amanda Ince (13)	102
Amy Kerrighen (12)	103
James Kent (12)	103
Sadikcha Malla (12)	104
Sam Kerr (12)	104
Racheal Barrett (14)	105
Kirsty-Ann Russell (12)	105
Callum Freel (13)	106

Eve Leonard (12)	107
Esther Coyte-Broomfield (13)	108
Edward Dale (12)	108
Joe Nash (12)	109
Christy Hause (12)	109
Jessica Ridgway (12)	110

Halesworth Middle School, Halesworth

Megan Wisdom (11)	110
Angus Mackay (11)	111
Sophie Rudd (11)	111
Philip Moyse (11)	112
Kelly-Ann Dilloway (11)	113
Stephanie Cadle (11)	114
Rebecca Bradshaw (11)	114
Polly Aldous (11)	115
Amy Woolnough (11)	115
Mikey Benjamin Shaw (11)	116
Tim Macardle (11)	117
Andrew Broadhurst (12)	117
Ryan Baker (11)	118
Erin Read (11)	119
Eleanor Brand (11)	120
Harriet Cox (11)	121
George Farrow-Hawkins (11)	122
Sophie Mills (11)	123
Leanne Mills (11)	124
Jessie Musk (11)	125
Michelle Stanborough (11)	126
Alex Reid (11)	127
Philippa Doran (11)	128
Kate Skingley (11)	129
Sophia Wilson (12)	130
Jennie Sherington (11)	131

Holbrook High School, Holbrook

Natasha Smith (12)	131

Honywood Community Science School, Coggeshall

Richard Hudd (13)	132
Molly Taylor (14)	132

Brittany Staples (15)	133
Lily Mihlenstedt (14)	133
Rowenna Butler (14)	134
Kirsty Mann (14)	134
Josh Howorth (13)	135
Robert Clark (11)	135
Becca Clarke (15)	136
Beatrice Morgan (15)	137
Jack Ardley (14)	138
Rachel Firth (13)	138
Jenifer Brazier (12)	139
Freya Stone (12)	139
Adam Clark (13)	140
James Smee (13)	141
Ella Neale (13)	142
Kieran Dixon (11)	142
Emma Cooper (13)	143
Emily Rose Clarke (13)	144
Kayleigh Webb (13)	145
Robyn Woodhouse (13)	146
Haydn Horner (13)	147
Katie Drakeford (14)	148
Joseph Baynham (13)	149
Jonathan Siddall (13)	150
James Rossington (13)	151
Grace Ellis	152
James Martin (13)	153
Elizabeth Beaver (13)	154
Verity Michie & Roisin Lightbown (11)	154
Holly Boag (11)	155
Victoria Nash (11)	155
Becky Drakeford (11)	156
Emily Eversden (12)	157
Duncan Mackay (11)	158
Francesca Burleton (11)	158
Emily Ambrose (11)	159
Miranda Elliott (12)	159
Rebecca Wingar (11)	160
Louise O'Reilly (11)	160
Bryony Butcher (11)	161
Kirsten Bradley (11)	161
Alice Tull (15)	162

Jennifer Irwin (12)	162
Katie Watts (12)	163
Tiffany King (11)	163
Becca Warder (15)	164
Harriet Moore (14)	165
Ben O'Connell (12)	166
Emily Mathias	167
Mark McFadden	168
Hayden Mihlenstedt (12)	169
Katie Gardner	170
Elizabeth Anderson (13)	170
Daniel Page (12)	171
Ross Baker (13)	171
Harry Sparkes (12)	172

Lancaster School, Westcliff-on-Sea
    Amy Mallandain, Christopher Reeves (14), Steven Holiday, Michael Kinsalla (15), Sarah Wingate (16), Wayne Clements, Mark Scott (17), Christopher Coates, Rocelle Vinluan (18) & Abbey Barton (19)   173

Manor School & Sports College, Raunds
Zoë Davis (15)	174
Megan Duggan-Jones (14)	175

Presdales School, Ware
Hayley Coen (12)	176
Ellie Parrott (11)	176
Bryony Ball (11)	177
Lucinda Green (14)	177
Luci Surridge & Rebecca Rasheed (15)	178
Natasha Burns (13)	178
Becky Buttall (15)	179
Keri Gilbert (13)	179
Alexandra Smith (12)	180
Emily Phillips (11)	180
Rebecca Hankin (14)	181
Laura Page (14)	182
Bianca Hill (11)	183
Kate Hinckley (14)	184
Alice Phillips (13)	184

Beatrice Smith (12)	185
Selma Michli (11)	185
Antonia Kitt (13)	186
Amelia Hicks (12)	186
Jessica Robertson (12)	187
Emma Davies (11)	187

Prittlewell Technology College, Westcliff-on-Sea
Olivia Mendez (11)	188

Royal Latin School, Buckingham
John Butcher (14)	188
Leah Woodford (14)	189
Natalija Carlsson (13)	190
Joe Lalor (13)	191
Olivia MacLellan (13)	192
Chloe Thomson (13)	193
Aidan Cooper (13)	194
Laura Jones (13)	195
Lauren Garner (13)	196
Tomas Goodgame (13)	197
Amardeep Bahra (13)	198
Jenny Raley (13)	199
Vanessa Charman (13)	200
Laurent Stephenson (13)	201
Charlie Calver (13)	202

St Mark's West Essex Catholic School, Harlow
Katie Reynolds (16)	202
Kelly Whalley (14)	203
Emma Bell (15)	203
Kayleigh Henderson (15)	204
Sian Gentry (13)	204
Fu-Wah Kwong (15)	205
Gregory Ashoori (14)	205
Toni Cleary (15)	206
Holly Bailey (15)	206
Claudette James (15)	207
Hayden Lester (13)	207
Dominic Steingold (15)	208
Matt Stent (15)	209

Ross Crisp (13)	210
Thomas Verbrugge (14)	210
Catherine Moranda (13)	211
Abe Pardue (14)	211
Tom Scanlon (13)	212
Lee Webster (13)	212
Niall O'Sullivan (13)	213
Zahra Ali (13)	213
James Smith (13)	214
Daniel Goddard (12)	214
Stewart Potter (13)	215
Danielle Murphy (13)	215
Elizabeth Shaw (13)	216
Sumana Begum (13)	216
Danielle De Cruz (13)	217
Thomas Day (13)	217
Katie Oliver (13)	218
Sarah Nulty (12)	218
Thomas Mintoff (13)	219
Georgia Gadsdon (14)	219
Theo Ancient (12)	220
Vanessa Heilbron (15)	221
Christopher Munden (12)	222
James Rose (14)	222
Rebecca Burnage (12)	223
Sarah Crehan (12)	223
Natalie Bell (12)	224
Esther Kingsmill (12)	224
Sarah Comerford (12)	225
Karen O'Callaghan (11)	225
Elise Turnell (12)	226
Callum Fitzpatrick (12)	227
Jade Clarke (11)	228
Louise Chapman (12)	228
Kate Allaway (12)	229
Robyn Fryer (11)	230

Soham Village College, Soham

Emma Garrett (15)	231

Southend High School for Girls, Westcliff-on-Sea
Rebecca Hamilton (15) 232
Sophie Bruce (15) 233
Sophia Bathgate (15) 234

The Colne Community School, Brightlingsea
Paul Watson (14) 235

The Perse School, Cambridge
Henry Beresford (12) 236
William Parker (12) 236
Max Hewitt (11) 237
William Raynaud (11) 238

The Sweyne Park School, Rayleigh
Daniel Vasa (13) 238
Bethany Elmer (11) 239
Michaela Galea (13) 240
Laura Thornton (12) 241
Rachel Steddon (11) 241
Chris Callahan (12) 242
Emma Tarling (12) 243
Rachel Hudson (12) 244
Lucinda Hughes (12) 244
Ben Cook (13) 245
Jasmin Wetton (13) 245
Nichola Todd (13) 246
Marc Wesley (13) 247
Nicole Evans (11) 247
Alex Blackmon (14) 248
Bradley Race (11) 248
Laura Walker (14) 249
Matthew Sharp (13) 249
Alex Furber (12) 250

The Poems

How's That For A Life?

Life is a bumpy road
Never easy, always rough,
If you go down you pull the strings to get back up,
Don't let life get you down,
Just get back up and go again,
Don't get depressed,
Bounce back up,
Fight till the end,
The end of your life,
Try and end on a high with your friends,
As a life without friends is not worth living,
If your life is full of death,
Move on from one place to another,
Don't be a criminal,
Love and live your life to the full.

James Thacker (13)
Attleborough High School, Attleborough

Home

I stand on this spot, looking out,
Summer breeze, it feels like
Electricity.
New taste in my mouth,
Dry like a dusty rag,
Brought on by this majestic view.

I stand in this moment, gazing.
The mountain's like a king
Watching his peasants.
The scene makes no sound
Still as a fallen tree
Soothing like water on a burn.

I stand here, peaceful, calm, careless
I marvel at the view
Finally I'm home.

Philip Starling (15)
Attleborough High School, Attleborough

Code Breaking

Silence, interrupted with a cough
Or a teacup's clink.
'He didn't make it.' He asked me 'Why?'
'Come on, eat something,'
Each word becomes an echo, unheard.

'Where's he gone now Mum?'
Perfect rounded tears roll down her cheek.

Now she's crouched over there, not aware.
Staring without cause,
Now she understands, she's realised.
Bye Dad, bye for now,
Hold the teddies, they're all you have left.

One day it'll happen to us all,
One day you'll miss me.
It's hard to understand what goes on.
Impossible to decipher the
Code of life and death.

Elisabeth Rickard (15)
Attleborough High School, Attleborough

Walk On Water

The smell of bitter salt air,
Curled into my senses like a forever-winding road,
The feeling of loneliness and independence,
Had never felt so good,
I wanted my eternity of overtaking,
Blue ocean to go on forever,
The tickling trickle of water running,
Through my toes like icing.
An excitement so unreal to mankind,
Cold pulsations ran through my blood,
Energy bursting out of me like an atomic bomb.

Paige Perfect (14)
Attleborough High School, Attleborough

Stuart's Nissan

Looking out at Stuart's Nissan, sitting in the yard,
Was enough to water the driest mouth, like a gushing waterfall.

It was a deep red like the bottom of a pool of blood.
The body kit, smooth and sleek as a flawless kick by
David Beckham.

The carbon fibre hood, although black as Satan's heart,
Was as inviting as the glowing, pearly gates of Heaven.
The golden-yellow neon under the car, at night,
Would be so bright, even the blind could see it.

The chrome rims and exhaust, glistened in the sun
Like freshly-polished crystal, after it is mined.
The windows, as dark as the sun is bright.
The speakers bounced like ping-pong balls in a blender.
Its engine roared like a lion, heard for miles,
Striking fear all the way.

Many times I thought it couldn't be any cooler . . .
However, Stuart's car became a legend, when he met,
'Pimp My Ride'.

Nicholas Colchester (14)
Attleborough High School, Attleborough

I'm Stuck!

I'm stuck for ideas,
My mind has gone blank,
Like a person wiping a slate clean,
My head is just spinning,
What topic can I choose?

I'm stuck for ideas,
Why can't this be easy?
Like it is for a bird to fly,
I want to write something
But I just don't know what.

Sarah Newby (14)
Attleborough High School, Attleborough

Love

When I saw you for the first time,
I felt a wash of excitement coming over me
Like a waterfall cascading down some rocks.
The feeling was alien to me,
I couldn't understand why,
I felt like that,
Until I saw you again.
You spoke with pure intensity,
Your lips a soft rose-pink,
Looked perfect on your picturesque face.
Now we're together I know what that unreal feeling was,
My heart telling me that one day we would be together,
It was telling me I was in love.
You're the last thing I think about at night
And the first thing I think about in the morning,
I will love you forever and always.

Amy Montgomerie (14)
Attleborough High School, Attleborough

The Moon

The moon is a headlight in the sky,
Fluorescent as lights in the classroom,
He appears now and then,
To watch over us, like his children.

The moon is as hard as nails but yet,
Gentle as a lily on water,
His surface is so rough,
With dish-like holes scattered like freckles.

So quiet is the moon, that it sounds,
Like the death of a deadly silence,
A smell of midnight air,
As it gently floats across the sky.

Laura Holland (14)
Attleborough High School, Attleborough

Helpless

Helpless as a leaf on the ocean, go with the tide,
Struggling to keep swimming, drowning inside,
Icy coldness grips your heart, like first fingers of frost,
Falling through the darkness, hopelessly lost.

Sadness flooding your lungs like a never-ending sea,
Trying to escape, failing to get free,
Don't think, don't feel, don't get too deep, it messes up your brain,
And when you stare at sunny skies all you see is rain.

The rest of the world's busy, but you just drift away,
Unattached, separate, going your own way,
Trapped inside a bubble, feeling totally alone,
Shut out of life, walk away on your own.

Sink right to the bottom, no further left to fall,
Crushed from all the pressure, feeling so small,
No more colours left to see, no more words left to say,
No lights shining in the dark, when everything looks grey.

Emma Dean (15)
Attleborough High School, Attleborough

The Match

The stadium fills as the match draws close,
The fans are ready for the highs and lows,
The weather is not good, it begins to rain,
Yet still, the ground's as packed as a peak-time train,
Sour defeat, sweet victory,
Tell me, what will it be?

The fans leave as the end approaches,
Some in cars, some in coaches,
Some are elated, some are sad,
Others are just downright mad,
Sour defeat, sweet victory?
Neither, it finished 3-3.

James Baldwin (14)
Attleborough High School, Attleborough

The Book Of You

You are like a book to me
A book I knew so well
Endless pages, thumbprint scattered
Each a memory, like fading ink,
Engraved into a book's bitter vellum.

You are like a book to me
A book I knew so well
Your mortal author may be dead
The one who breathed each letter of life
Unknowingly scrawled or neatly scribed.

You are like a book to me
A book I thought I knew
A year since your ending began
Slowly each page of memories
Is written in an unaccounted tongue.

I can't read it, the words are lost,
I feel them escaping, sense them fade,
Until there's only a soulless, tatty cover
Your name lightly pencilled onto
The bitter vellum of the only page.

You are like a book to me
A book I know so well
Each page I have re-written
Hazy thoughts and half-remembered days
Not quite true but the sun shines every day
On every word and every page.

Elanor Hall (14)
Attleborough High School, Attleborough

The Life And Love Of The Potato

First it's a potato,
Shoved into the ground,
Then there are many potatoes
And that goes round.
The first sight being
A rickety rusty barrel
Losing control at an unthinkable speed
Down an unknown hill.
Then you see spots,
Spotty like a teenager being brutally attacked
By unpleasant, unattractive acne.
When holding this vegetable,
It feels like sandpaper,
Which has been used time and time again.
However it's colourless
Like a glass of fresh ice-cold water.
The taste of the potato sends some to Heaven,
For those going to Heaven,
Their mouth waters
Like a shaggy dog dribbling, after a needed thirsty drink.
You can feel the emotions a potato feels.
When cutting through it viciously
You can feel the pain tearing at your heart.
But nobody really cares,
For the potato is their evening meal
From the ground to the plate,
That's the life and love of the potato.

Sian Duval (15)
Attleborough High School, Attleborough

As Sweet As Summer Should Be

A distant memory,
A golden sunray,
A long shadow dancing
Across the way,
As sweet as summer should be.

A child's laughter,
A fluttering breeze,
A warm sunshine evening
Beneath the trees,
As sweet as summer should be.

A shining rainbow,
A lifetime of play,
A star-studded night
As daytime slips away,
Everything is happy and free,
As sweet as summer should be.

Amber Bradbury (14)
Attleborough High School, Attleborough

Bitter-Sweet

This orange was as detailed,
As the thoughts in my mind,
As it melted in my mouth with this sensuous joy,
Crying as the juice oozed out of its untouched skin,
The smell was as wild as a silver skinned fish,
A taste so strong I could feel it sticking to the roof of my mouth,
As it smoothly slid down the back of my throat,
I could feel its texture on my tongue,
Like the mornings unbrushed teeth,
Oh and a taste so sweet like candyfloss pulled fresh
From the machine,
This orange is by far the best I have ever seen.

Rachael Dickenson (15)
Attleborough High School, Attleborough

Frosted

Glowing windows, frosted with ice,
Glossy berries, nestled in wreathes,
Delicately wrapped presents under trees,
Eagerly waiting to be revealed,
Candles glow like the moon at night,
Illuminating things that lay in the dark.

The crisp snow falls from up above,
Covering everything in sight,
The scent of mince pies fills the air,
Whilst mistletoe is hung in homes,
The days are short and soon it's night,
Everyone is tucked up tight.

Heather Briggs (14)
Attleborough High School, Attleborough

Burning, Burning!

It is burning in the night,
It is losing its own fight,
It is trying but not winning,
It is crying but is willing,
It is dead but never gone,
It is ash but not for long.

Hannah Chenery (12)
Attleborough High School, Attleborough

Viewing The Spectacular

I sit there in anguish,
Silence, like the aftermath of a battle.
Thump . . . it is hit with sheer passion, angled aggression.
The unbelievable has commenced, he's outdone himself this time
. . . Jubilation!

Sean Craemer (16)
Attleborough High School, Attleborough

Chocolate (A To Z)

A t first I start with one bite
B ut that just might
C reate a need
D epending if I plead
E ven more
F or more
G enerous amounts
H eavenly accounts
I ntense my mood
J ust for food
K eep me happy
L aid back, not snappy
M elting on my lips
N ot going on my hips
O range, mint or white
P leasure in my sight
Q uestion me not
R espect the whole lot
S mooth and creamy
T asting dreamy
U tterly delicious
V ery nutritious
W ell that's not true
X L bars I'll eat a few
Y ou ask what gets me in this state
Z ero in on chocolate mate.

Evelyn Edwards (12)
Attleborough High School, Attleborough

Grass

Grass
Just grass
It grows, it lives, it dies
It's just grass, pink or otherwise
It's always there
Everywhere
It's part of life you see
But when it's gone
It leaves a gap
A gaping hole
Just like that.

It's missing
It's gone
There's something just not right
It's wrong
No green or pink or brown or grey
Just barren landscape
Like a cloudy day.

And then it's back!
The world lights up
The sun comes shining through
It's back! It's back!
The world makes sense
And that's what makes you realise
Just how much it means to you.

Jennifer Davey (14)
Attleborough High School, Attleborough

My Favourite Place

All my cares are lost at the beach;
I leave them back at the dunes,
Go for a stroll with my dog and his ball,
At peace, at one with the sand and the shore.

Gulls fly freely over our heads
Further in land for colder months,
Whilst a seal bobs up and down in the sea
Like a velvety buoy, just floating around.

We love it here, my dog and I,
A place to feel free and breathe;
There is plenty of space to run around,
For the dog, at least; maybe not for me.

I prefer to stand at the edge
Where the sand meets the water,
Yet it never rests from relentless waves,
Like a hundred people hushing and sighing.

After a run and a play and a swim,
A towel awaits back at the car,
That tireless dog refuses to come,
But joins me at last, and we can go home.

Hannah Clifford (14)
Attleborough High School, Attleborough

The Melon

Mmmm, more colours than a tropical sunset,
Mmmm, as sweet as a child's smile,
Mmmm, the succulent squelch of bare feet on wet sand,
Mmmm, as smooth as your childhood space hopper,
Mmmm, the smell of a thousand trees,
Mmmm, in front of me it sits, like an old lady unable to move,
Mmmm, 'The melon'.

Sam Bodmer (14)
Attleborough High School, Attleborough

Bullying

Like a tiger hunting
A deer fiercely,
Boy bullying young girl
And made her cry.

She went to her teacher
And told her all,
Her teacher told him off
She was left alone.

Emily Follows (12)
Attleborough High School, Attleborough

The Bully

The bully walked down the aisle
As evil as the Devil,
As rotten as a rat,
He nearly hit me with a bat,
His sinister smile spread a mile,
I could not stand it, *the bully!*

Jack Lebbell (12)
Attleborough High School, Attleborough

Dog

My lovely dog called Spike,
As fluffy as a short cuddly toy,
As fast as a leopard,
As playful as my brother.

As black as darkness,
As smelly as a frozen fish,
As black as a tyre,
Like a leopard in the wild.

Benjamin Brown (12)
Attleborough High School, Attleborough

Anger Finding Life

Anger is a fiery life
It boils and bubbles
Rising heat
The resented things.

We feel it
Know it
Some embrace it
Some just fear it.

Our feelings rage
Our hearts confused
We don't know
What to do.

Yet ever and anon
We find our way
Stumble on a hidden path.

Find the door
Open to another world
We open our eyes
To another world we never see.

For life a winding road
We walk on day by day,
Find a new path to lead,
To find the future days.

Thomas King-Fisher (15)
Attleborough High School, Attleborough

Cat

As friendly as my mum's smile,
As bright as the shining sun,
As small as the leaning grass,
As gentle as my mum's driving.

Daniel Forde (12)
Attleborough High School, Attleborough

Gymnastics

Bars, beam, floor and vault,
You lose points if you make a fault.
Competing is my favourite thing,
About gymnastics even when you don't win.

On the bars you swing and twist,
When you're getting on, you have to be swift.
Circle up, jumps and spins,
It's taking part that counts and I won't give in.

Beam is next and it's sort of hard,
To cartwheel along it, when it's sweaty as lard.
Tuck jump, straight jump, arabesque,
Competing is like a humungous test.

Floor is easy if you know,
To stand up straight and point your toes.
Round off, chassey forward rolls,
We have to work hard to reach our goals.

Vault is last you have to jump,
Hard on the springboard to come down with a thump.
Handstand lay flat, straddle on,
Now we've got to wait to find out if we've won.

It's the end now, I came third,
Now when I round off, I fly like a bird.
I've learnt a lot about gym today,
No more competing until next May.

Sophie Barker (13)
Attleborough High School, Attleborough

Dog

My dog is as friendly as a dolphin,
His fur as black as a hole,
As cute as a rabbit and hamster,
As fast as a cheetah.

Kenneth Williams (12)
Attleborough High School, Attleborough

Rafting

The expectation was amazing,
The river was as wide as the Grand Canyon,
And as dark and deep as a black hole,
Dark, grey rocks were sticking up like old gravestones,
Piercing the surface like a needle through the skin.

The water was as cold as ice cubes,
Splashing in my face like wedding confetti,
The rapids sound like crashing thunder
And were as fast as a Formula 1 car,
The raft bobbed about like a seagull on the waves.

Feeling as though I had no control,
Paddling hard like a gold medal rower,
Arms aching like I'd lifted a tonne,
The thrill of the ride like a roller coaster,
Came to a halt, as suddenly as it began.

Kerri Morgan (16)
Attleborough High School, Attleborough

She

She wished she was a bird to fly far, far away,
Everyone thought she was crazy because she did not want to stay,
She wished she was a bug, so that she could escape,
She didn't care what she looked like in any form or shape,
She wished she was a tiger, prowling through the snow,
But her wishes never granted with her feeling so very low,
One day people woke up to find that she was gone,
They say she couldn't cope with things,
Like she was being held on puppet strings,
Still she had no family, no flowers on her grave,
No friends either even with all the love she gave.

Sam Pickles (14)
Attleborough High School, Attleborough

My Favourite Things

Spare rib
As fresh as a newborn lamb,
As precious as a bone to a dog,
And as lean as a taught muscle,
As red as an embarrassed face.

Bike ride
As calm as a gentle river flowing,
As fast as a bullet ripping through the air,
As peaceful as the fog in the graveyard,
Wind rushing through the rider's hair like a wave.

Music
As rhythmic as a metronome,
Loud enough to make the speakers bleed,
As fast as bullets from guns,
As multi-cultural as Britain.

Tom Bulmer (12)
Attleborough High School, Attleborough

Poetry

Who's to say what poetry is?
Why is it me you have to quiz?
Poetry is a special thing,
It can make you laugh, dance or sing,
Poetry is a thing you read,
Poetry is a special thing, you see,
It is anything you want it to be,
There are no guidelines, rules or laws,
Only if you don't write do you have flaws,
Who's to say what poetry is?
Why was it me you had to quiz?
I wrote this poem easily
And it's from my heart.

Matthew Rogers (11)
Attleborough High School, Attleborough

Work

The smell of sweet cash in my hand,
The meaningless smile I display.
The chaotic banter that fills my ears,
As I wipe back the tiredness from me.
I begin to wonder when will the clock strike nine?

My eyes become sensitive to the city of lights,
But I carry on working,
Smiling and asking how I can help.
I no longer see their faces.
Every face emerges into a ticking clock.
What only feels like frozen droplets of sweat appear on my skin.
The sickly smell of food overwhelms my senses.

As I realise the time . . .

My ears become no longer blocked by the chaotic banter.
The tiredness no longer drowns me.
And the smile is almost nearly sincere, people's faces re-emerge.
As I realise it's almost nine o'clock,
My shift at work has finally finished.

Natasha Doyle (16)
Attleborough High School, Attleborough

Chocolate

Parents, teachers, social workers,
Say they want children to be happy,
Then they give us healthy foods,
And boring drinks with zero fizz,
If they really meant their words,
They'd give us Coke and chocolate spread,
Chocolate is our favourite food,
It puts us in a happy mood,
So try to understand kids' needs,
Stop feeding us those plates of weeds.

Ashley Gowland (12)
Attleborough High School, Attleborough

That Noisy Fireman's Bleeper

Beep, beep, beep,
That small box stuck to his hip.

Beep, beep, beep,
24/7 it never shuts up.

Beep, beep, beep,
How can a box that small sound so loud!

Beep, beep, beep,
There it goes again.

Beep, beep, beep,
The nightmare started.

Beep, beep, beep,
Every time.

Beep, beep, beep,
Three more beeps and he's gone.

Beep, beep, beep,
Not even a goodbye.

Alicia Lacey (12)
Attleborough High School, Attleborough

Animals

There are so many animals in the world,
The cat, the mouse, the toad,
Some people hate them and some people love them,
The horse, the tiger, the elephant,
Some are big and some are small,
The ant, the giraffe, the dog,
Some are very, very cute and some are ugly,
But they're the
Greatest
All the same.

Beth Reeve (11)
Attleborough High School, Attleborough

What Is Poetry?

Poetry is the spark of the fire
And how the flame starts small
And ends as a small flame.

Poetry is the sea bashing against the cliffs,
Coming in and out and never stopping.

Poetry is all the colours in a rainbow,
Bright in the sky,
Sun or rain.

Rachel Fleming (11)
Attleborough High School, Attleborough

TV

TV makes you into a zombie
That believes anything it tells you.

TV makes you do things
You normally wouldn't do.

TV normally has a million and one
Channels and there is still nothing to watch.

TV . . . well TV is great!

Luke Downs (13)
Attleborough High School, Attleborough

Poetry

Birds are cheeky and loveable,
They are always up to mischief,
Back and forth, back and forth across
The branches of the trees,
Constantly chirping,
Birds are wonderful, full of surprises.

Sofia Dodson (12)
Attleborough High School, Attleborough

How I Love Chocolate

Chocolate is so smooth and sweet,
My life's favourite desire,
There are three main types,
Milky, white and dark.

Milk chocolate so divine,
Texture so rich and creamy,
Without chocolate,
How would I survive?

White chocolate so deluxe
So thick and pure just like snow,
Looks so innocent,
Makes me feel so guilty.

Finally dark chocolate,
The flavour so rich and strong,
Wish I could eat it,
Without growing fat.

Michael Edghill (11)
Attleborough High School, Attleborough

Football's Crazy

Football's crazy,
Football's mad,
Anyone's better than your rubbish dad.

Football's smashing,
Football's great,
You can't even beat my mate.

Football's the best,
Of course it is,
It's the only sport which is the biz.

Football's the thing which cheers me up,
Because I haven't got a pup.

Charlie Joe Burnage (11)
Attleborough High School, Attleborough

My Shampoo

Opening the lid of the shampoo
Smells of a bed of roses
Comes rushing out like fireworks
Putting shampoo on your dirty hair
Massaging it into your hair
Sticking your hair together
Slowly taking you to paradise
Suddenly coming back to Earth
Trying to turn the taps on
Covering the taps with scented foam
It's either too hot or too cold,
When it gets to temperature,
You add the water to the shampoo,
Slowly washing the foam away,
Until the water turns clear,
Washing the taps with running water,
Turning the taps off when finished,
Your hair is all clean and fresh now.

Kayleigh Briggs (14)
Attleborough High School, Attleborough

My Cat Boo
(In memory of my cat Boo)

My cat Boo was my best friend,
My cat Boo would sit on my bed for hours and hours,
My cat Boo was like a warm blanket with a soft purr,
My cat Boo was purr-fect!
My cat Boo died, I lost my best friend that day.

My cat Boo can purr and sleep for hours and
Hours on a fluffy white cloud,
That's where she is now, high up in the sky,
My cat Boo makes the sun shine brightly,
That's why I love my cat Boo so much.

Charlotte Willis (11)
Attleborough High School, Attleborough

What Is Poetry?

What is poetry? What is poetry?
Is it everything?
Is it nothing?

Who is poetry? Who is poetry?
Is it God?
Is it you?

Why is poetry? Why is poetry?
Is it fun?
Is it boredom?

What is poetry? What is poetry?
No one knows,
No one knows.

Dominic Hazell (11)
Attleborough High School, Attleborough

Fantastic Place

There is a place called Rome
It's nothing like home
It's fun in Rome
Old buildings and shopping
Always stopping
I'd love to go to Rome.

Savanna Kmecik (13)
Attleborough High School, Attleborough

A Dog Poem

My dog is as small as an ant,
My dog is as fast as a jaguar,
My dog is as cute as a soft toy,
I love my dog.

Joe Smith (12)
Attleborough High School, Attleborough

She Was Very Special To Me

My great grandmother was special to me,
Because she was the only one I had,
She was calm and gentle,
And always loving, but very special to me,
She had a letter from the Queen,
When she reached 100,
And sadly died when 101, but was very special to me,
But she was great,
And was lucky to live that long.

Joanna Slater (11)
Attleborough High School, Attleborough

What Is Poetry?

Poetry is the world of tomorrow,
Poetry is like a goblin's sorrow.

Poetry is like a fast car,
Even if it doesn't go far.

Poetry can mean anything at all,
It can even be one foot small!

Matthew Freeman (11)
Attleborough High School, Attleborough

What Is Poetry?

What is poetry? Where is poetry?
In your heart or thrown with a dart?
Is it a deep, dark cave,
Or a bright beaming sun?
Does poetry make you jump with joy,
Or left with the old broken toys?

Georgia Whyman (11)
Attleborough High School, Attleborough

Australia

The beautiful trees and plants in blossom,
In a place we call Glossom,
The cockatiels chirp in song,
As the cockatoos and macaw squawk all day long,
I'm so glad I'm moving here soon,
I lay waiting staring at the moon,
Until the day comes,
I'll sit and practise my aussie hums.

Luke Hughes (11)
Attleborough High School, Attleborough

The Jungle

At first it may seem unappealing,
Standing there, wet and steaming,
But the jungle is special, a wonderful thing,
Animals standing, sitting, doing everything,
Plants growing towards the light,
Seeming as tall as the stars.

So now dear friend, I hope you're converted,
From buying mahogany chairs.

Thomas Curtis (11)
Attleborough High School, Attleborough

Kung Fu Hamster

Soft and furry like my cat,
My Kung Fu hamster,
He waits on my desk ready,
For me to play with him,
When I'm around I watch him,
Do a funny dance,
He used his brown nunchucks,
To kill anything in his path.

Adam Turner (12)
Attleborough High School, Attleborough

My Family

My mum loves dogs,
My dad loves frogs.

My auntie Nick is like a fairy,
My uncle Chris is very hairy.

My auntie Val loves her rum,
My uncle John has a very big bum.

My auntie Kay likes lots of honey,
My uncle Bruce is very funny.

My auntie Cathy has hair that's curled,
My uncle Rob travels the world.

My cousin Laura is good at drawing,
My cousin Hayley is good at yawning.

Then there's me
Weird, wonderful and perfect
In every way!

Not!

Lorna Allen (12)
Attleborough High School, Attleborough

Dolphins

Dolphins think like humans,
They like to splash and swim,
They like to have lots of fun,
If they were human they
Would be professional divers,
The water is their home,
Where they do all sorts of things,
They care about children very much,
Adults too,
Everyone should love dolphins,
Because they love you.

Jasmine Card (11)
Attleborough High School, Attleborough

A Beautiful Game

I can hear the crows' cries ringing in my ear,
'Deeeno, Deeeno, on the ball City!'
The scent of freshly mown grass, hot dogs
And strong tobacco fills my nostrils.

Players bombing down the wing; tackles flying all over the place,
Suddenly the crowd screams again deafening me, 'Shoot!'
What is this object flying towards me?
A sphere roughly the size of a melon.
It's the ball, the opposition comes darting towards me.

I hop over him, I've done him like a kipper,
A Maradona here, a step over there,
Instantly *bam!* in the top corner,
The next thing I know, the whistle screeches in my ear,
Once again the crowd roars, 'Deeeno, Deeeno,'
It echoes on until next Saturday.

Thomas Saunders (12)
Attleborough High School, Attleborough

What Shall I Put In The Poem?

Your poem can be anything,
Anything you want,
The sun or the moon
Or the sky or the ground!
It can be joy or frowns,
Love or hate,
Sadness or gladness,
Naughty or nice!
Sugar or spice!
It's your poem,
Not his or hers,
Yours,
Do what you want with it.

Sophie McKenna (11)
Attleborough High School, Attleborough

My Poem About A Girl Called Amanda

She is bubbly and full of glee,
She often stays round mine for tea,
She loves animals, anything,
Even a bird who can't sing,
She has a dog who she takes for walks,
She imagines that he can talk,

She has birds, about fifteen,
They're all different colours; yellow, white, green,
She has a guinea pig, a rabbit too,
I've been to her house and it's like a zoo,
She is my cousin and my best friend,
I hope we're together right till the end.

Michaela Fiddy (12)
Attleborough High School, Attleborough

Evy The Sherbert Lemon

S he is mad
H er name is Speedy Evy
E vy is like a sherbert lemon,
R ough in the middle
B ut smooth on the outside
E veryone has their opinions
R ed hair for the sunset
T ime goes on hip hip hooray!

L ovely though she is
E vy is very weird
M aybe she is abnormal
O r maybe she's just different
N o matter what, we love her!

Sophie Binks (12)
Attleborough High School, Attleborough

Chocolate

A thing I like is rich and creamy,
But it makes me feel so dreamy.

Chocolate is the thing I like,
Down the shops I go on my bike.

Eating too much chocolate will make you fat,
First thing in the morning you'll look like Garfield the cat.

Greedy and greedier you will become,
Huge and enormous will be your tum.

Indigestion will be the next stop for you,
Just after you have finished four hours on the loo.

Kit-Kat and Crunchies,
Lion bars and Munchies.

Munch, munch, munch,
Not crunch, crunch, crunch.

Orange chocolate is the best,
Plain chocolate I detest.

Quietly munching throughout the day,
Right up until bedtime if I get my way.

Stuffed full is my fat belly,
Time to watch Red Dwarf on the telly.

Unexploded is written around my belly button
Victor my doctor says I'm a glutton.

Wash it all down with lashings of pop,
Xmas means my supply of goodies won't stop.

Yes, the teachers all say my homework is late
Zip down to the fridge for more chocolate for me and my mate!

Victoria Moore (12)
Attleborough High School, Attleborough

Tin And Bin!

Today we'll be mates
And the day after that
Until we graduate
If we do that.

Today we'll be mates
And the day after that
Until we get husbands
If we ever do that.

Today we'll be mates
And the day after that
Until our in-laws die
Thank God for that.

Today we'll be mates
And the day after that
Until we are grannies
In our old woolly hats.

Today we'll be mates
And the day after that
Until we're lil' angels
No one's gonna believe that!

Tyne Courtney & Bri Murray (12)
Attleborough High School, Attleborough

On The Beach

On the beach I hear:
Seagulls squawking like sirens,
Children wailing for ice creams like dolphins,
Waves rolling on the shore like the schlosh of sand
being dropped into a bucket of water,
Traffic whizzing by like . . . traffic.
But the thing I hear most . . . my dad snoring on his lounger.

Christina Martell (12)
Attleborough High School, Attleborough

Troy

As gold as the plate
the king dined on
Stone like the muscle
of the body
The city so grand
and full of great fear.

A battle as big as the beach
where it was fought.
Arrows so many, they blacken
the sun's rays of light
Archilles the great hero
cuts through the battle
like Moses through the
Red Sea.

Jacob Peckett (12)
Attleborough High School, Attleborough

Mystery Girl

Her long blonde,
Swaying in wind,
Five months past and what has she done?
Her long blonde hair has turned into a bit of fun.

A layer here, a layer there,
A bronze here, a chestnut there,
Her blonde hair is now
A luxury supermodel look.

Everyone loves it even me,
The hairdresser and the family,
As for my mystery girl,
Has just turned *eighteen!*

Rebecca Etteridge (12)
Attleborough High School, Attleborough

Life

Life is like a rocky roller coaster,
Up and down, round and round,
Boring bits, exciting bits, fun bits too,
What's around the corner?
I don't know, do you?

Life is like a steep mountain,
Meeting new things along the way,
Easy bits, hard bits, stumbling all the time,
But when you reach the top,
Death do us part.

Victoria Watling (12)
Attleborough High School, Attleborough

What Is Love?

Love is your best friend and worst enemy,
It can be an angel's blessing or a devil's curse,
Love can bring a cupful of joy or a bucketful of hate,
It can plaster a permanent grin or everlasting frown,
All love has ups and downs,
But everyone has it, even you.

Kerry Cross (12)
Attleborough High School, Attleborough

Death

The darkness has taken you to a better place.
At last I don't have to see you lying in pain.
Although you have taken a special piece of my heart with you.
Every day is another filled with grief.
The tears I cry for you are wishes that one day you will return home.
I wish I could see you once more.
I feel so alone.

Hollie Judge (13)
Attleborough High School, Attleborough

The Sea's Transformations

At night the sea wakes up as a lion,
Roaring and raging at anyone who dares go near its territory,
Desperately trying to pounce over the boundary wall,
Dragging anything that meets with it to a close end.

But in the day the sea is a gentle pussycat,
Pouncing lightly back and forth,
Playfully teasing the glistening blanket of sand,
Its gentle salty spit splashes out,
As it wraps itself around people's feet and purrs soothingly.

Though sometimes after a great shake,
The sea is taken over by a tsunami dragon,
A cacophony of sounds is heard,
Then over the boundary wall it goes,
Eating up everything in its path,
Spitting out mountains of salty water,
Causing nothing but devastation and loss.

But once the icy cold death waters calm down,
The sea is back to being a gentle pussycat,
And a trapped lion at night.

Anna Blaser (12)
Attleborough High School, Attleborough

Behind The Piece

Horse hair dipped in careruleum-blue,
Swooped across the age
Pastel smudged all over hands,
Pithalo, emerald, sage.

Dead trees scraped on rough canvas,
Screech, scrape, score.
Mars black, process and paynes grey,
As detailed as an apple's core.

Bethany Gibbs (12)
Attleborough High School, Attleborough

Untitled

Big dogs,
Small dogs,
Fat dogs,
Skinny dogs,
Brown, black, gold or white,
Alsatian, Labrador, Staffie and Rottweiler,
A dog is a man's best friend,
You hate to be apart,
A dog is someone you can talk to,
To a dog you can open up your heart.

Josh Whiterod (12)
Attleborough High School, Attleborough

The Shot

The bullet was racing towards me,
pushing the air aside,
a train going full pelt down the track,
one million pounds of metal in a small chunk,
my emotions ran wild.
I stared down the barrel of my metal murderer,
scarlet-blood rushed through the piercing in my chest,
a bright light shone in my eye.

Jason Sturman (12)
Attleborough High School, Attleborough

Breaking My Ankle

I was rollerblading with my friends
They were driving me round the bend
Suddenly I fell to the ground
Crying, screaming not very proud
Breaking my ankle
It was like sharp knives cutting into my skin.

Kathryn Mather (13)
Attleborough High School, Attleborough

Ever Heard Those Names?

The artists who shaped
The world today,
Are not often talked of
I'm sad to say.
Leonardo da Vinci
And Abraham Darby,
Panamarenko
And Brunel.
Ever heard
Those names
Before?
Not many have.
Even though they
Are the names
Of the artists who shaped
The world today.

Joshua Bunn (12)
Attleborough High School, Attleborough

The Bog Brush

It sits there looking innocent
And clean, just brand new,
But when you put it in the bog,
It gets all clogged with muck.

This muck, we know just what it is,
And it happens every day,
We cannot help what humans do,
And how we lose the waste.

That's what the bog brush's job is,
To clean up all the scum,
We all know what it is,
And that it comes out of your . . . !

Ashley Davis (12)
Attleborough High School, Attleborough

Best Friends

Best friends are like one single, colourful, bright pink flower
In a field of dead green weeds.
So prominent yet so easy to miss.
So rare, once they are gone they are gone.
So if you see a colourful bright pink flower
In a field of dead green weeds,
Pick it,
Hold it,
Keep it.
Don't let it go,
It might be your only one,
So look after it.

Molly Naldrett (12)
Attleborough High School, Attleborough

Nintendo DS

As cool as ice
Like a box of fun
Shiny like a silver bar
As good as life
Like being in a dream
Like a machine that takes away boredom.

Ciaron Amos (14)
Attleborough High School, Attleborough

My Dog

Golden like melted cheese
My lovely dog, Amy
As friendly as my old dad
As bright as a yellow sun.

Amy Horth (12)
Attleborough High School, Attleborough

Is It So?

A piece of art,
A red rose,
Love.

The sun shines brightly
On the world,
Why?

Is it for us to go through life
With love around us
And hate behind us?
Yes.

We go through life like a race
And when we reach the finishing line
It's time to say goodbye.

Josie Pinnock (13)
Attleborough High School, Attleborough

Spaghetti

When I had my plate of spaghetti
It looked like a plate of worms
It looked like it was moving
But it was very nice
And that was my tea.

When I had my plate of spaghetti
It tasted like home-made pasta
And it smelt like roses
That's what I had for tea.

When I had my plate of spaghetti
It was as long as the blue sea
It was as bright as the sun
As yellow as it too
And that was my tea.

Alice Fletcher (13)
Attleborough High School, Attleborough

The Sweet Shop

Cherry Drops
Like little red jewels
Like circle-shaped buttons
As red as a red petalled rose
As sticky as a bee's golden honey
As round as a pumped-up football.

Skittles
Like different colours of the rainbow
It's like tasting the rainbow
Soft-centred and sour circles
As round and as colourful as a beach ball.

Chris Cromack (13)
Attleborough High School, Attleborough

Bright Lights

The bright lights of the city
Are always so pretty
With thousands of shops
Millions of tops
There's always something to do
In the bright lights of the city.

Ciaran Long (12)
Attleborough High School, Attleborough

Rainbow

R ain gently pitter-patters on the ground
A s people strut around the high street
I n the shops people wait
N ow the rain begins to stop
'B rilliant!' the people cry as the sun comes out
O h the people come to shop under the light drizzle
'W ow!' the people cry gazing at a beautiful rainbow.

Josh Downes (12)
Attleborough High School, Attleborough

Chavs

Chavs are as hard as a piece of paper
They wear their hats like a feather on their head
All they do is smoke and make fights
But they are not as hard as my four-year-old brother
The bling on their fingers just makes girls go,
'Oh they look fit, no they're Chavs!'
Their Nike trainers cost £90
But they look like they are from a charity shop.

Jason Miller (13)
Attleborough High School, Attleborough

Untitled

It's as boring as listening to opera
or watching paint dry

It's as boring as playing chess
or reading a book

It's as boring as daytime television
or watching the fishing channel

It's as boring as boring gets
it's boring, it's school.

Luke Mitchell (13)
Attleborough High School, Attleborough

The Moon

T he moon shines with all its might
H is rays of light light up the night
E very house in the town can see it bright

M oon is surrounded by stars that look like tears
O n which they glisten like glitter
O n the horizon the sun is coming up
N ow the moon has gone till tomorrow.

Kirsty Clarke (13)
Attleborough High School, Attleborough

Life

Not a day goes by
When someone doesn't cry
A day in which something happens
When you lose someone
It sucks up all your fun
You have to say goodbye.

Your love has gone
It is your darling son
What will you do?
Ask yourself is it really true?

Your mother has gone
She was all you needed in one
Love is important.

Kim Wild (14)
Attleborough High School, Attleborough

The Wonderful Game

As tense as a guitar string
Is the sparkly sun when clean
As fun as playing on your PS2
As bad as killing each other
Hit the ball as hard as towers falling
Hit the net like cars hitting each other.

It makes you cheer so much
Like an eclipse when dirty
As fun as playing on your PSP
As bad as stabbing someone else
Tackle the player as hard as planes hitting
Hit the back of the player like boxers.

Robert Warren (13)
Attleborough High School, Attleborough

The War

Marching men go into battle,
Widow wives left to graze the cattle,
Happy families soon to mourn,
All because of this stupid war.

The sound of horses galloping away,
Warriors say they'll be back . . . some day,
The generals shouting out commands,
Wives and children held in arms.

Sparks are flying from their swords,
Men are crying to their lords,
These brave men are dropping like flies,
Now appearing are black skies.

We see two generals without a grin,
But with these wars, no one seems to win.

Shaun Banham (12)
Attleborough High School, Attleborough

Sloth

A sloth I am, slow and tired
Eating leaves at my desire
An eagle waiting for the catch
Sloth vs eagle, not an even match
The reeking stench of rotting fur
I will die tonight that is for sure
The eagle flying swift as lightning
Rips out my stomach, me not fighting
Falling to the forest floor
Landing with a thump, blood and gore
Life ebbing away feeling sore
Not enough energy, even to crawl.

Andrew Johnson (13)
Attleborough High School, Attleborough

Football

Kick a football up in the air,
You head it hard and it ruins your hair,
Back of the net 1-0,
Or a cheeky back heel,
What a save by the keeper,
Or a back four, defensive sweeper,
What a pass,
Your team said it was class,
You love playing football all day and night,
You can't kick with your left foot but you can kick it with your right.

Danny Moore (12)
Attleborough High School, Attleborough

School

It is so boring, like being tortured
Like being banged up for no reason at all
Like sitting in a cell for five long hours
Like waiting in the dentist's; I'm so bored
Like waiting behind an old granny in a car
Like travelling on a school minibus
Like travelling five hundred miles in a car
School is boring, like watching golf on telly.

Sean Robinson (13)
Attleborough High School, Attleborough

Rain

Rainy days won't go away,
Sunny days have gone for good.
Rainy days so we can't play,
Sunny days were so good.
Rainy days just go away,
So sunny days are here for good.

Rosie Waugh (13)
Attleborough High School, Attleborough

Untitled

The night sky so dark and cold
Stars brightening up the world
Dark clouds suffocating their light's safety
Leaving the world in blackness
Scary figures left to linger in the shadows

Cars whizz past bringing a small light to the land
Black heavy clouds drowning the earth below
Drenching each of our souls
Black is the night, light is the day
When will my sorrows go away?

Laura Gipp (13)
Attleborough High School, Attleborough

Untitled

An autumn day begins
With brown, red and yellow
Leaves float calmly to the ground
Crunch, crunch, crunch
Kids running round and round
Till they're dizzy and mad
The autumn day ends
With a pinkie sky.

Lauren Rapley (13)
Attleborough High School, Attleborough

Chocolate

The sight of my kitchen floor tiles,
The sound of a crack or a split,
The taste of cocoa beans,
The smell of hot chocolate,
The rough feel of the top
And the soft feel of the bottom.

Hannah Goward (11)
Attleborough High School, Attleborough

Persecution

Blood on our hands
What have we done?
Has mankind been reduced to this?
Stealing, killing, raping
What have we done?
Has mankind been reduced to this?
Why have we destroyed our humanity?
Why have we pillaged and perged so?
Has mankind been reduced to this?
How did it come to pass?
Pain has wrought our lives so
Blood has met blood
Lives have been destroyed viciously
How did it come to this?

Norman Stillwell (16)
Attleborough High School, Attleborough

The Unknown

She sits quietly by the shimmering blue sea
and purring her dark melody.

Under the awakening full moon she thinks of me
however far away, wherever I may be.

She wishes that I could stay here with she
who sits in the 23rd hour, under the bare oak tree.

The crystals in her eyes are beginning to be
nothing more than a distant memory.

This girl may seem rough but she did have a key
but alas the key is no more because with me
it drowned in the shimmering blue sea.

Hermione Howson (13)
Attleborough High School, Attleborough

See You Now

When I saw you standing there,
I couldn't move, I had to stare,
It was special, it meant so much to me,
If only I meant as much to you.

She reminds me of someone else I knew,
The times gone by, memories still hurt,
Why can this not be different?
Why do I fear the same result?

Excuse me chap, is my hair alright?
Excuse me chap, does my breath smell?
Excuse me chap, do I look good in the light?
Excuse me chap, you ask who these efforts are for, I'll never tell.

She is the light that could help me back,
Always dreaming, never living,
Don't worry chap, there's always tomorrow,
Until, oh, she's interested in that other lad now.

Well, the final result has come,
As I said it would,
And even though I still love you,
It still hurts to walk home alone,
    y'know?

Elliott Heading (17)
Attleborough High School, Attleborough

Ladybirds

Spotted, like a young child with chickenpox,
Crawling along the long green lush lawn,
Like a bright red Smartie being carried along
By hungry carnivorous ants,
With small, tiny black spots like freckles on a pretty girl,
The ladybird flies like a gliding bird,
It's silent, it cannot be heard,
The ladybird, the ladybird.

Emily Broad (13)
Attleborough High School, Attleborough

My Auntie's Tomatoes

My auntie's shiny tomatoes
the colour is lush red
so extremely gorgeous
so wonderfully delicious

The taste is terribly scrumptious
as tasty as can be
I love my auntie's tomatoes
I really, really do.

Jessica Sacharczuk (13)
Attleborough High School, Attleborough

My Day At The Beach

The waves crashed on the ocean floor,
I could hear the rustling of the palm leaves,
My small hands cold as an icicle,
I was shivering inside my body.

As the day went on, the atmosphere got warmer,
My feet were no longer numb,
I realised that it was nearly time to go,
Come on Mum, I'm about to run.

Ryan Saunders (13)
Attleborough High School, Attleborough

Bridesmaids

The church was cold and grey like a winter's day
The sparkling white dress was like a swan
Swimming gently across the calm lake
Excitedly walking towards the vicar
Felt like winning the lottery
Confetti fell to the floor
Like feathers on a carpet.

Gemma Snelling (13)
Attleborough High School, Attleborough

My Dog

Yellow like vanilla ice cream
Playful as a puppy
Hole digger like a rabbit
Fat as an old cat.

Hairy like a gorilla
He can be lazy
As friendly as an old lady
He chases the cats.

Carla Moore (11)
Attleborough High School, Attleborough

Toyota Supra

Custom like a private jet,
As light as a F1 car,
Powerful like thousand horse,
Noisy like roaring lions.

Carbon bonnet light like hair,
White like a layer of snow,
As beautiful like a rainbow,
Smooth as melted chocolate.

Philip Mickleborough (11)
Attleborough High School, Attleborough

Cut Grass

Smells as fresh as the morning air
Falls to the floor like feathers
Like a feathery bed
Soft as a fluffy pillow
Birds swoop down to find juicy worms
Neatly strewn over the floor
Like the blanket of feathers.

Mark Anderson-Wilson (13)
Attleborough High School, Attleborough

A Daughter's Hidden Love

I have suffered, long and hard
I have cried, hour after hour
Resisted the urges to find you
To hunt you down
Like a redcoat on horseback

Waiting for a moment
A moment that will never occur
Like a pig with its wings
Awaiting a time that is only best forgotten
Because once the hope's gone
The dream dies too

Unanswered questions
Swirling in my young mind
Like oil upon the water's glassy surface
Fighting back the tears like rising floods
When I have no mop
Holding onto what little I have of you

So many times I've wanted to scream out loud
Lash out at the arms holding me down
That bind me as tight as bandages
Over wounds that will never heal
Enclosed in my lonely tomb
Only the pain preserved

But how will I know when you've gone?
Will you ever return for me?
Lonely tears fall over the thought
Like the blanket pulled over the face
I have to move on, or I'll never learn
But what's the point in hiding love in a crevice?

Sarah Pickersgill (16)
Attleborough High School, Attleborough

Pagani Zonda

The shiny chassis sparkling
Like a big star in the night sky.
The noisy engine grunting
Like a worn-out tractor engine.
The sound of the roaring, powerful engine
speeding past me like a lion's roar
calling for the rest of the group.
The speed is like a huge cheetah
running desperately after its prey.
The size of the marvellous fast car
is like a full grown rhino pushing its way
through a stampede.
The sparkling alloy wheels
dazzling the shiny, big moon.
The speedy car is like my heart beating away.

Ryan Moore (13)
Attleborough High School, Attleborough

Paddy

March 17th, Paddy abandoned on the streets of London
A frightened bundle of fluff.
Rescued by a kind person
Who delivered him to Battersea Dogs Home.
My father said, 'We're off to London.'
He didn't say the reason why.
I hoped it would be a surprise for me.
I just couldn't wait to see.
When we arrived at the home my excitement grew.
I couldn't wait and see.
In the corner of the room was the frightened bundle of fluff.
Now he was my dog Paddy!

Katherine Humphreys (11)
Attleborough High School, Attleborough

James Bond

With a black jacket
With a hard punch
With a twinkle in his eye
With a high-tech car
With a gun he carries round
With a shoe full of equipment.

He slowly stalks his prey

With night vision glasses
With a silent motorbike
With a girlfriend like he never had before
With secret places
With people to be his slaves
With a whole world to save.

Toby Clements (11)
Attleborough High School, Attleborough

Champions

The night was as tense as a violin string,
when the players entered it was a stampede.

The noise was like a tsunami,
as they kicked off it exploded.

It was the last penalty,
the ground was shaking like a bass drum.

It went in, the crowd went crazy
like the people in hurricane Katrina.

They celebrated into the night,
the bars rang with the sound of delight.

Louis Gyde (13)
Attleborough High School, Attleborough

Love

Love is like great joy,
It brings you lots of feelings,
Love looks like bright red,
It smells like lovely roses.

Love can feel so soft,
It can bring you very close,
Love will touch your heart,
Love can sound like a heartbeat.

Love can make you cry,
Love can be a lovely thing,
Love can be so kind,
Love can be so wonderful.

Abby Richards (11)
Attleborough High School, Attleborough

Fragile And Powerless

The old man fell to his seat
Like an old fragile china pot
He hit the chair with great impact
He smashed with great defeat

He braced to get off his chair
With spectacular despair
When the man stood so, so tall
He smiled never before

He walked with inspiration
So slow but happy inside
When he reached his destination
His blood ran with sensation.

Sam Lawrence (13)
Attleborough High School, Attleborough

Animals

Soft as a baby chick
Smelly like perfume
Nasty as a slimy slug
As noisy as a wolf howling
Light as a summer's day
As happy as a monkey
Dirty like a wet, muddy field
Cute like a small baby.

Chloe Babel (11)
Attleborough High School, Attleborough

Spain

As salty as a bag of chips
The sand was as soft as cotton
I could just taste the smell of salt
The sun was as hot as an oven.

My feet just sink into the sand
Sandcastles in the distance
The sun is as golden as honey
The waves crash onto the shore.

Persia Winter (11)
Attleborough High School, Attleborough

Arai

My cute and fluffy cat,
Pounding in my messy bedroom
She flops into my lap
Her eyes gleam like large diamonds.

Looking up into my eyes
She pushes her head into my hand
Her nose is icy cold
As I hear a silent purr.

Serena Suggitt (11)
Attleborough High School, Attleborough

Great White Sharks

The long body
Teeth as sharp as flint
Vicious and mean
Always on a hunt

Seals are so scared
The whole ocean freaks
Be careful at sea
Kelp moves out of the way.

Connie Holliday (11)
Attleborough High School, Attleborough

My Cat Smudgy

My cat called Smudgy,
Is as black as the night sky,
With paws white as snow,
Eyes shining like emeralds.

Fur soft like velvet,
Graceful like ballerinas,
Claws as sharp as knives,
A heart as big as the sky.

Hannah Carr (12)
Attleborough High School, Attleborough

A Beach

As gold as a new made coin
As soft as the fluff of a pillow
The sea as blue as the sky
As warm as a bath or cold as ice
As salty as a salty pot
As refreshing as a lovely sleep
As glistening as the stars
As gritty as a full bowl of salt.

Jamie Potts (11)
Attleborough High School, Attleborough

The Thing

I wandered in the park one day
To go play on the swings
I fell into a great big hole
It left me quite amazed.

It was round and deep like a well
When there it was; the thing
It left me in a state of shock
To see it coming near.

Danny White (11)
Attleborough High School, Attleborough

Fox

As red as a flame
As furry as a cushion
Smells like rotten meat
A tail as furry as a brush.

A small animal
A cold-blooded animal
As quick as a hare.

Jamie Henderson (11)
Attleborough High School, Attleborough

Ferrari Enzo

Ferrari Enzo, red, black and yellow.
Blink and you will miss.
Ferrari Enzo, the best car I know,
Creamy leather seats.

Ferrari Enzo, have you ever heard?
Did you know it flies like a bird.
Ferrari Enzo, gorgeous as can be,
As you know it looks just like me.

Edward Tyce (11)
Attleborough High School, Attleborough

Watching Arsenal

As I hear the Highbury crowd roar
I jump with joy
But soon realise it's only half-time.

A sea of red shirts
Shout at the biased referee
There he goes again.

Chris Merry (11)
Attleborough High School, Attleborough

Benson

Soft fur around a silky nose
Whiskers tickling my face
Bright green eyes glow in the dark
Ears like pointed knives.

Soft pink paws upon my cheek
A silver and cream tabby
A long tail towering above him
A sweet miaow from Benson.

Taila Hunt (11)
Attleborough High School, Attleborough

My Pets

Pets are really cute
Pets really want to come home with you
Pets are really sweet and you know it
Pets are really cuddly.

Pets are really nice to have
Pets keep you happy
Pets are really nice to play with
Pets are happy to look after you.

Keeley Hoyte (11)
Attleborough High School, Attleborough

Liverpool Poem

Football is great,
Football is cool.
I wanna be number eight
For Liverpool.

I'm only eleven,
Gerrard's twenty-five,
I would be in Heaven
If my dreams came alive.

I wanna be red
And score for my team,
It's in my head, it's only . . .
It's only a dream.

If I go to Anfield
I'll be famous and delighted,
I'll run onto the field
And be extra excited.

The Kop's gonna roar
With Skipper on the ball,
And yes I can score,
I'll be proud and tall.

Today as I sit
And pencil this poem
I look at my kit,
I'm only at home.

Jack Skipper
Attleborough High School, Attleborough

Pets

P erfect and cute animals
E ven when they die, and
T hey will always be in my heart
S afely locked in my memories.

Emma Seville (11)
Attleborough High School, Attleborough

My Brother - The Dog

My brother is a dog
He puts toys in his mouth
Just like a dog
He eats dog biscuits
And puts dog bones in his mouth
Just like a dog
He always dribbles
Just like a dog
But most of all I love him very much
Just like a dog.

Tiffany Bolingbroke (11)
Attleborough High School, Attleborough

Monty The Cat

My cat called Monty,
Has pure white socks,
He takes after his mother.

She is thin and slow,
She likes hunting mice,
She kills them,
Then brings them into the house.

Polly Fyson (11)
Attleborough High School, Attleborough

The Punk

He liked to go to the bar in his Jaguar.
He hung around with a punk and never got drunk.
He hated all the tourists and picked on all the posers
And heck! he hated surprises!

George Harrison (11)
Attleborough High School, Attleborough

My Dog's Life

My puppy is very cute
Its name is called Stella,
She's got a black eye.

Demi Long (11)
Attleborough High School, Attleborough

Jellyfish

Relax and stretch,
Push, got to move
Don't touch me
Or I'll sting you!

Georgina Pipe (13)
Braeside Senior School, Buckhurst Hill

The Tree Protector

Diamonds falling from the creamy sky
Umbrella protecting the sad children
Children crying, wanting to play in the rain.

Vanessa Hoh (12)
Braeside Senior School, Buckhurst Hill

I Can See!

I can see a garden full of snow
I can see trees and bushes
I can see people, but not me!

Sanya Akhtar (12)
Braeside Senior School, Buckhurst Hill

Snow Angels

Pearly white costumes,
Drifting down,
Never to be seen again.

Helen Walker (12)
Braeside Senior School, Buckhurst Hill

Snow Blizzard

Snow is falling like blossom,
Coming down as fast as a roller coaster,
Rolled out like a long, fluffy carpet.

Shana Patel (12)
Braeside Senior School, Buckhurst Hill

The Snowdrops' Celebrity

Fans bright crowding to their saviour,
Their heads drooped as if they were no greater,
They are gone when the sun shines down so strong.

Lydia Smith (12)
Braeside Senior School, Buckhurst Hill

A Carpet Of White

There are fairies falling on the ground
With a carpet of white beneath them
They sit there and dream away.

Lucy Benham Whyte (12)
Braeside Senior School, Buckhurst Hill

How The Garden Grows!

Have you ever stopped to look?
Can you feel the nature?
You may just become hooked.

Iesha Agyemang (12)
Braeside Senior School, Buckhurst Hill

Nature Awakes

Nature awakes from a long, long sleep.
Shoots stretching their arms in motion,
While they praise the sun.

Gabrielle Compton (12)
Braeside Senior School, Buckhurst Hill

Patterns Of The Tree

The rough bark of a tree reminds me
Of hard, tough, scaly skin.
The pattern of the bark, like veins.

Samantha Staab (12)
Braeside Senior School, Buckhurst Hill

Picking Colours

I feel like gardening today
Picking all the rainbow colours
Red, orange, pink, green, yellow, blue
And purple flowers.

Emily Benham Whyte (12)
Braeside Senior School, Buckhurst Hill

Whee!

Creaking of the stairs.
Stationary.
Screeching of the slide.
Whee!
Whistling of the wind.
Tummy turns.
Cool breeze!
Up . . . down
Touch the sky . . .
Touch the ground!
What a day!

Rebecca Bushell (13)
Braeside Senior School, Buckhurst Hill

Fun While It Lasted

Snowflakes dancing in the sky,
Roll a ball
See how high it can fly.

It's getting colder,
The sun's getting low,
It's time to return home,
Now the snow will slowly go.

Isabelle Docker (13)
Braeside Senior School, Buckhurst Hill

Snow Drifts

Snow looks like diamonds.
Twisting and falling from the sky,
Like graceful dancers, dressed in white.

Alexandria Martin (13)
Braeside Senior School, Buckhurst Hill

Washing Machine

The washing machine goes,
Round, round, round,
With a leap and a
Bound, bound, bound.

Along with the sounds,
Splash, splash, splash,
And the buttons go
Crash, crash, crash.

When it all slows down,
Stopping the sound,
The clothes all stop,
No longer going round.

Rebecca Lee (13)
Braeside Senior School, Buckhurst Hill

Memories Of Snow

As we look back on history
Each memory glides down
And a white blanket puts them to sleep.

Nicole Abbott (13)
Braeside Senior School, Buckhurst Hill

Snowdrops In A Winter Breeze

The tree like Mother Nature
the centre of attention
little angels bow to her feet, as they fall.

Holly Chapman (12)
Braeside Senior School, Buckhurst Hill

Winter

As winter gets colder,
The water begins to freeze.
As winter gets colder,
There comes a bigger breeze!

Winter is so cold,
I wrap up warm.
Winter is so cold,
I'm in a freezing storm!

The snow is falling,
There's snowmen being made.
The snow is falling,
Snow ploughs are getting paid!

Winter's nearly over,
The snow begins to go.
Winter's nearly over,
The grass starts to show!

Skye Jacobs (14)
Braeside Senior School, Buckhurst Hill

Rebirth Of An Egg

Sitting here,
In a freezing cold fridge,
With all my mates.
Suddenly, a burst of light
And I am moving towards a black hole.
Crack!
My head has been split,
A whole new me is born,
With my pale skin
And yellow hat.

Natalie Stone (13)
Braeside Senior School, Buckhurst Hill

Snow

Cold and damp and white is snow,
Flowers, birds and plants must go,
Like a spreading, shiny sheet,
Making patterns with your feet,
Settles on your window ledge,
On a tree or on a hedge,
Snowflakes falling from up there,
To keep warm takes a lot of care,
Shovelling snow from your path,
Snow fights really make you laugh,
Skis and sledges pass and go,
Oh I really love the snow,
And tomorrow it will go.

Sophie Goodhew (13)
Braeside Senior School, Buckhurst Hill

Rabbit Meets Car

Hopping along the side of the road,
No one there.
Hopping across the road.
A car.
Staring at the car.
Car brakes, car swerves.
Bang!

. . . Car meets tree.
Rabbit hops off.

Chloe O'Connor (13)
Braeside Senior School, Buckhurst Hill

The Fear Of A Snowdrop - Haiku

Tree won't let them go,
Baby snowdrops in the snow,
It's too dangerous.

Sitara Ali (12)
Braeside Senior School, Buckhurst Hill

Winter

The lake is freezing,
Snow is falling,
Slowly to the ground.
Smiles are fading,
Light is leaving,
Winter's here.
It's finally found.

Christiana Bourne (13)
Braeside Senior School, Buckhurst Hill

Frisbee

Round and round,
Spinning into oblivion.
Round and round,
Don't stop me.

Round and round.
Catch me.
Round and round,
Can't stop spinning.

Francesca Higgins (13)
Braeside Senior School, Buckhurst Hill

Ice Servers

The icy daggers stare down at me
With the bats as their slaves,
Watching the trespassers enter their cave.
The icy blizzard outside chases me through the entrance
With the wind at its heels.
The shadows enclose me and my torch is not working.
The darkness eats away at me.
I'm finished, diminished by the army of the Arctic.

Alexandra Jack (13)
Braeside Senior School, Buckhurst Hill

Swim Like A Fish

OK!

Warm up
Eight lengths

Ready . . . go!

1, 2, 3
Breathe

Faster
Got a beat
Fish and chips

Fish and chips
Breathe
With tomato sauce
Breathe

Fish and chips
Breathe
With tomato sauce
Breathe

End of length
Slow down
Tumble turn

Out of tumble
Get a beat

Crisps and dips
Breathe
Crisps and dips
Breathe

Last length
Slow down
Nearly there

Stop!

Jenna Brown (13)
Braeside Senior School, Buckhurst Hill

Attack

I walk slowly down the gloomy road,
Concentrating about my surroundings.
I am alone and it is dark.
But I have a dark scary feeling
Inside me that someone is watching me.
I stop. I look around me but all I can see
Are the street lights on.
I keep walking, thinking of where to sleep.
Next to the bins . . . no, too dirty.
Next to the park gates . . . no, I may get caught.
In the alley . . . yes, excellent.
I walk into the alley, I lay my blanket on the floor
And sit on it with my back against the hard, spiky wall.
I look up and stare at the beautiful sky:
I can see the moon. It looks like a beautiful jewel
Lying on a black velvet background.
In my head I ask God why He chose me.
The silence is broken,
I hear something shuffling near me.
I look. I can see a figure of someone dark.
The night is too gloomy to see him.
I run. I can hear his footsteps
Crunching the snow behind me.
Crunch, crunch, crunch, *bang!*
I feel something sharp go in my back.
Within a few seconds, I drop on the floor.
All I have to face now is the judgement from God.
I sleep peacefully . . .
With my soul floating
Higher . . . higher . . .

Shehana Udat (13)
Braeside Senior School, Buckhurst Hill

Fox

A red blur, a fox
I watch in awe
As a defenceless fox
Runs for his life
Thunder, hooves
A chase, a race
A beat of a heart
Running, jumping
A race against time
Gallop, gallop
As fast as you can
A pant, a sniff
The scent of blood!

Lucy Brunt (13)
Braeside Senior School, Buckhurst Hill

The Jungle

The scent of ripeness,
The flowers and fruit
All remind me
Of the jungle.

Over the acres of fruit trees
You can hear the booming of a million bees.
All reminds me
Of the jungle.

Honey-coloured sunlight
Hitting the sand.
All reminds me
Of the jungle.

The birds singing in the trees
And the gaudy butterflies flutter by.
All remind me
Of the jungle.

Toni Gidney (13)
Bury St Edmunds County Upper School, Bury St Edmunds

In The Jungle

In the jungle it's not what it seems,
One minute silence, the next there's a scream.
That awful noise that will make you run,
That horrible noise that comes from a gun.
The blood that pours out and down,
Then the monkey's dead on the ground.
The hunter appears out of the trees,
In the jungle, it's not what it seems.

Ashley Bugg (13)
Bury St Edmunds County Upper School, Bury St Edmunds

Flames

Within the flames you see the light,
In the shadows of the night.
Dark and cold quickly flee,
With the dancing flickers of thee.
Sometimes feared, mostly loved,
Watch them burning through the wood.
Flames dance high, flames dance low,
At the end, just embers glow.

Alex Henshaw (13)
Bury St Edmunds County Upper School, Bury St Edmunds

A Shark

A shark swims through the sea
Like a knife through butter,
Its big mouth covered
By its sharp, razor-like teeth.
It kills its prey in one big bite,
Blink and you will miss it.
It swims back in the big black sea.

Ryan Bailey (13)
Bury St Edmunds County Upper School, Bury St Edmunds

Blackwater

B right, shimmering sun beams down
L ovely lying in the sun
A lex come and rewinds it all
C ruel, crying Alex feeling sorry for himself
K neeling, begging for forgiveness,
W hingeing and whining as Brodie says, *'No!'*
A ngry Alex is ashamed,
T rying to make Brodie happy,
E vil Alex has no luck,
R uining Brodie's holiday, what a shame.

Kersha Haynes (13)
Bury St Edmunds County Upper School, Bury St Edmunds

The Island

The white sand is glistening in the sun
And the blue sea's waves lapping against the shore.
The young children playing happily, having fun.
No one can really ask for any more.
Ralph and Jack ordering around,
The big scar where the crash happened,
But now there is a sound of happiness
And sadness is cured.

James Scott (13)
Bury St Edmunds County Upper School, Bury St Edmunds

A Firework

Boom! I am a firework,
I zoom through the sky.
The boom is like a gunshot
When I burst.
The sparks are like a sparkler.
I get set off in November.

Sophie Nichols (13)
Bury St Edmunds County Upper School, Bury St Edmunds

I Am An Outsider

I have no people to surround me
I have no friends or family
Because I am an outsider

Whilst I sit alone in my cardboard box
Children shout whilst throwing rocks
Because I am an outsider

As I stare up at the dark, dark sky
I feel I have no longer till I die
Because I am an outsider

My life is not like any other
I have not a sister or a brother
Because I am an outsider

People run straight past me without a simple sound
Just a little giggle that still hurts inside
Or a horrid frown

Because I am an outsider.

Jo Jones (13)
Bury St Edmunds County Upper School, Bury St Edmunds

Black Water

B rodie has plans for the summer holiday,
L ost by Alex coming to stay,
A nxious was Brodie to get rid of Alex,
C ancelling his plans with his friends,
K eeping control of his anger,
W ishing Alex would be gone,
A lex could not swim, so Brodie tried to teach him,
T aking Alex to the river, trying to reach him,
E xtremely angry when he saw Pauline with a boy,
R iver was rough and took one life; maybe two?

Sarah Button (13)
Bury St Edmunds County Upper School, Bury St Edmunds

Everywhere The Scent Of Ripeness

Everywhere the scent of ripeness,
The booming of a million bees,
The touch of soft soil on my feet,
A great tree fallen across the floor.

Creepers woven into a great big mat,
Acres of fruit trees across the island.
With a pair of gaudy butterflies flying high above,
Seeing flowers and fruit everywhere.

I walk down to the soft sandy beach.
It glistens in the warm, bright sun.
The soft sound of waves against the shore,
Going gently in and out.

Everywhere the scent of ripeness,
The booming of a million bees,
The touch of soft soil on your feet.
Why can't I just stay?

Adam Redfern (13)
Bury St Edmunds County Upper School, Bury St Edmunds

Moon

There is a moon that comes up at dusk
And goes down at dawn.
It is big and bright and it looks like a ball
Floating in the big black sky.
At dusk it's like a balloon that has been let free
And it pops up to show its shine.
At dawn it's like it's being pulled down on a piece of string
And then it disappears until dusk again.
Shine, shine, shine.

Rebecca Guy (13)
Bury St Edmunds County Upper School, Bury St Edmunds

The Dead Island

The waves crash and roll,
Tossing debris onto the sands,
As the strange voices of the wind
Eerily whisper words of death.

At the top of the hill,
A ghost town lies,
A relic of the past,
Secret and silent.

In the gnarled, dead trees,
There are strange inscriptions,
While in a burial cave,
Gruesome corpses lay.

I'm scared, so scared,
Terror has enveloped me,
Like night over day,
As I wait and wait for someone to find me.

Laura Anders (14)
Bury St Edmunds County Upper School, Bury St Edmunds

Hands

I can move all over the place.
I can make a weird sound.
I can move all around.
I have long fingers to help me pick up things.
I have long fingers to feel things.
I have lots of joints to help me move.
My life ends when your life ends,
And when your life starts,
My life just starts.
I move when you are first born.

Samantha Ashford (13)
Bury St Edmunds County Upper School, Bury St Edmunds

Candyfloss

Round and round the fairground,
By the swinging chairs,
Is the colourful candyfloss stall.
Let's go over there.

It looks all sticky and sweet,
I want some for a treat.
'Mum, can I have some please?
Would I get some if I got down on my knees?
Can I have some Mum, please?'

Bethany Raper (13)
Bury St Edmunds County Upper School, Bury St Edmunds

Bullies

B ehind me there they are
U nder the table watching me
L ooking at me, watching every move I make
L eaning over me as they are taller than me
I s it because I'm ugly, small or maybe because
   I'm from another country?
E nemies with me but I don't know why
S cared of everything and what they are going to do next.

Sammy Boscheck (15)
Bury St Edmunds County Upper School, Bury St Edmunds

The Jungle Nightmare

I am in a jungle, dark figures leaning over me.
I can see a dark ship out at sea.

I see that I am not alone.
From the ship I hear an awful drone.

I start walking away over the sand,
But I see a shadowy hand.

Adam Farrant (14)
Bury St Edmunds County Upper School, Bury St Edmunds

Hide-And-Seek

Closed in, where no one can find me,
Smiling, hearing voices passing by.
Darkness, only silhouettes are visible,
Hide-and-seek, such an easy game to play.

They've given up because they couldn't find me.
It is time to make my hiding place known.
I know what to do, I'll jump out and scare them.
I can't, somehow the door is locked shut.

Waiting for my friends to hear me screaming,
Banging on the door which is shut tight,
Sitting feeling sick and claustrophobic,
Hungry for the food I know is out there.

Lonely, will anybody find me?
How long will I have to stay in here?

Emily Ruddock (13)
Bury St Edmunds County Upper School, Bury St Edmunds

The Island

The calm sandy island with coconut trees,
Hundreds of plants and bushes with berries.
The soft sandy beaches,
With squidgy pink peaches
And lukewarm water lagoons.
In the dark green forest looms
The acres and acres of hundreds of trees,
A scent of ripeness goes past in the breeze.
In the distance comes the booming of bees.
Just below the dark canopies,
Riotous colours where flowers collide.
Behind creepers, animals lie.
Honey-coloured sunlight from up in the sky.
A flock of butterflies goes flying by,
Birds and bugs and fish in the sea.
The sun-filled island left to be free.

Hattie Wright (13)
Bury St Edmunds County Upper School, Bury St Edmunds

The Jungle

What can you see?
The bees buzzing in the trees.
Where are the birds?
Are *they* in the trees?

What can you feel?
Can you feel that breeze?
The beautiful butterflies,
High up in the sky.
Can you fly as high as the butterfly?

What can you hear?
I can hear the animals on the ground,
Eating the fruits all around.
What's that wind in the trees?
Did you feel that enormous breeze?

Tatiana Golden-Collinson (13)
Bury St Edmunds County Upper School, Bury St Edmunds

Stranded

A glowing, burning, tremendous plane crash.
Up shoot the flames, down falls the ash.
Dead people here, dead people there,
Not enough bodies to send out a flare.
Searching the wreckage thoroughly through,
Picking up tools, food and water too!
Indulging so deep, so deep in the gloom?
I might be gone, vanished with a boom!
Searching for shelter and natural supplies,
Anything I find I'll take, it'll be mine!
But still I stay alert, aware,
Anything could possibly be lurking in there.

Ashley Hardy (13)
Bury St Edmunds County Upper School, Bury St Edmunds

My Island

Somewhere out there
In the middle of the sea,
Bathing in the sun's glare,
There might be an island.

On this land
Lie the remains
Of a city
Called Atlantis.

Tall pillars of stone,
Gold and silver,
Reach towards the sky,
Walls lie tumbled and jumbled,
Strewn across the floor.

Plants climb and clamber
Through the empty wreck,
The deadly silent presence
Of the people who aren't there.

Beth Newton (13)
Bury St Edmunds County Upper School, Bury St Edmunds

Heaven Or Hell?

Smash, the sound of the fallen tree.
Pitch-black is all I can see.

I am enclosed, I can't breathe,
The sand and the grit makes me heave.

I don't know how I am going to get out.
No one can hear me, even if I shout.

The roar of the booming bees,
Swarming among the trees.

I came to a place where the sunlight fell,
This place is Heaven, not Hell.

Jordan Wiemer (13)
Bury St Edmunds County Upper School, Bury St Edmunds

The Island

I am on a desert island,
I am not alone,
I am on a beach.
Listen to the ocean.

I am on a desert island,
I am not scared,
I am foraging.
See the beautiful trees.

I am on a desert island,
I am calm,
I am finding water.
Smell the sweet scents.

I am on a desert island,
I am worried,
I am helping others.
Taste the tropical fruit.

I am on a desert island,
I am not afraid,
I am planning.
Feel the smooth, dry sand.

I am on a desert island,
Who I am, you know.
What am I doing here?
I'm not here, it's *you!*

Josh Foster Brown (13)
Bury St Edmunds County Upper School, Bury St Edmunds

A Nightmare

As I close my eyes and drift away,
I wish I could have a peaceful night.
No chasing, no murder.

I'd rather dream of happy thoughts
Than nightmares of unreality,
But for some reason, that doesn't happen.

I'm in a world that seems familiar,
Although I don't recognise anyone,
No one seems to know me either.

Busy people cross the street,
One of them seems familiar.
Who is it? Where are they from?

He is a funny little character,
Running around on his six feet.
I realise in a flash that it's Stitch.

He comes towards me, hobbling along,
His face shows anger.
He speeds up, he's after me.

I start to run but I don't seem to move,
He is on my tail, chasing me.
What is he after? What does he want?

His sharp blue talons
Draw towards my neck.
I scream for help but no sound comes.

I lie in my soft warm bed,
Drenched in sweat,
Wishing I could have had a peaceful night.

Élodie Limer (13)
Bury St Edmunds County Upper School, Bury St Edmunds

New Discovery

Three pairs of eyes glaring out of the window,
The excitement running through our bodies,
Finally there.
Small feet pattering along the grey concrete,
Hitting the hot burning floor,
The distant noise of lapping waves, drawing nearer.
Golden sand in-between our toes,
The wind blowing through our hair.
Watching the rough sea, controlling the beach,
The pebbles looked angry as they flung back and forth,
A place full of emotion and feelings.
Once catching the waves,
We walked back through the sticky sand.
We picked up the ocean pearls
And left our new discovery.
We moved on to our last location,
Our hands gripping onto one another,
From a distance we heard cries of laughter.
We saw the tall rides in front of us,
The lights shone like multicoloured stars,
As we walked around we watched children
Carrying candyfloss, big pink balls of wool.
As our eyelids began to drop we left
The magical place we had discovered,
Ready to return next year.

Millie Packer (14)
Bury St Edmunds County Upper School, Bury St Edmunds

The Island

Trees swaying, sun shining, waves lapping,
Paradise . . .
Birds singing like heavenly angels,
Beautiful . . .
Dolphins leaping with joy, monkeys shrieking with praise . . .
Praise for this island, 'tis a wonderful place!

Jack Kimber (13)
Bury St Edmunds County Upper School, Bury St Edmunds

The Jungle

Creepers dropped their ropes,
footprints in the soil,
unexpected pale flowers,
the open space of the jungle.

Tall canopy,
tall trunks,
little ferns,
aromatic bushes.

Booming bees,
the scent of ripeness,
bowl of heat and light,
handful of ripe fruit.

Candle buds,
large trees,
prickly bushes,
acres of fruit trees.

Keiran Wingfield (14)
Bury St Edmunds County Upper School, Bury St Edmunds

Island Poem

Seeing the view of the remote tropical island
from above was amazing, you could see the golden
sand circle round the island, with the coral sea
trickling back and forward on the golden sand.

Arriving at this tropical hotel that is a calm,
relaxing hotel for two weeks with a peaceful
environment, also with a luxurious sea view
from the balcony that is just amazing.

After a while we went down to the sandy beach,
where the blistering sun was shining at its brightest.
We played volleyball for a while, then we just sat back
and relaxed on the remote tropical island.

Daniel Kemp (13)
Bury St Edmunds County Upper School, Bury St Edmunds

Falling

Higher and higher I climb
I am only nine
I can see everything around,
The crumbled leaves fall to the ground.

Higher and higher I climb
My friend looks like a dot
I take a big leap
And I hang on for my life.

Higher and higher I climb
Crack goes the tree
My grip's losing the hold
My arms start to unfold.

Lower and lower I fall
The ground rushes to meet me
Too quick to jump away
I break the branches with my fall.

Simon Johns (14)
Bury St Edmunds County Upper School, Bury St Edmunds

The Beach

Dancing upon the golden sand,
The sun beating down on my sparkling hands,
Pink petals graciously lining the sea,
It may not be yours but it's my cup of tea.
But here the cocktails are lined up till nine,
The bartender's wailing, 'I'm tipsy from mine!'
And then the dusking night draws to a close,
But not before the 'Hula girls' strike one last pose.
The locals fall down getting a face full of sand,
As the moonlight gleams down on my sparkling hands.

Rachel Cox (13)
Bury St Edmunds County Upper School, Bury St Edmunds

The Prey

The green leaves were our camouflage
Up the tree we hid
Speckled bark at our feet
We quietly filled our guns
Not daring to give a shudder
They approached from below
As the hunters, and we were the prey
Then it was our time to become the hunters
The guns had been fired
The bottles had been emptied
What a mistake that was
We were back as the prey
Fleeing for our lives
As frightened and startled rabbits
But it was too late
The bitterness of the water tore through our clothes
And it was all over
We were, and will always be, the prey.

Alicia Hardy (14)
Bury St Edmunds County Upper School, Bury St Edmunds

Sitting On The Edge Of Paradise

Sitting on the edge of paradise,
Flower and fruit grow together,
Trunks bear popping flowers,
Honey sun spills over like a waterfall,
Creepers drop and curl joining into each other,
Bright fantastic birds worship the sky with their cries!
The blue sea breathes in and out,
Sitting on the edge of paradise!

My world is shared with my family,
Scrunching golden sand between our toes,
Draping hands into the sea,
Sitting on the edge of paradise!

Meg Shorten (13)
Bury St Edmunds County Upper School, Bury St Edmunds

Scooter

Yes! Thanks Mum!
I had just got my new scooter.
As we got to the top of the hill,
I told my mum I was going down.
Whee! This was really fun!
But as I was getting faster and faster,
Too fast for my liking.
My brakes weren't very good,
As it was only a little scooter,
It wasn't designed to go that fast.

I was scared.
I was starting to swerve, and kept swerving,
Then, as I just got to the end,
I flew straight over the handlebars
Crash!
Ouch! My bag had flew over my head.
I had grazes all over my arms and hands.

Gemma Candy (14)
Bury St Edmunds County Upper School, Bury St Edmunds

Beautiful

Acres of fruit trees blossoming with colourful fruit;
Overhead tall canopies where eager creepers shoot.
A fallen tree, sprouting little plant ferns,
Flaunted red and yellow sprays make your eyes churn.
Unexpected pale flowers revealed by honey coloured sunlight,
Soft brown soil dampened by the night.
A scent of ripeness spilled throughout the air,
Handfuls of ripe fruit; apples, bananas, pears.
Gaudy butterflies flutter, elegantly to rest,
As darkness falls the moon shows its best.

Juliet Mills (13)
Bury St Edmunds County Upper School, Bury St Edmunds

The Island

I saw the plane with one wing
I saw the other across the beach
I saw the volcanoes
Standing like a monument in the middle.

I heard the screaming of people
I heard the sound of wildlife
I heard the sound of the sea lapping
Against the rocks far far away.

I smelt the salt air from the sea
I smelt the burning of the plane
I smelt the volcanic scent in the distance
I saw, heard and smelt a disaster.

Aiden Hughes (13)
Bury St Edmunds County Upper School, Bury St Edmunds

Jungle Colours

Riotous colours,
strike my eyes,
bright fantastic birds
and gaudy butterflies!

Acres of fruit trees,
woven creepers,
surrounding all of the
tiny sleepers!

Honey-coloured sunlight,
glowing on the sand,
a bowl of heat and light,
all over this beautiful land!

Scarlett Brabrook (13)
Bury St Edmunds County Upper School, Bury St Edmunds

The Tramp

Sleeping in the alcove on the street,
Dirty like a rat,
Lonely, cold and quiet,
An outsider,
Friendless - he is alone,
Homeless,
Torn boots,
Tatty clothes,
Sitting now - on a bed of cigarette packets,
A hat now on the path with a few coppers,
Cuddling up to his tatty, dirty-coated dog,
Waiting . . . waiting . . . waiting
Only if he had proper shelter,
Another cold night on the way,
Again,
Waiting . . . waiting . . . dreaming . . .

Emily Victoria Webb (13)
Bury St Edmunds County Upper School, Bury St Edmunds

The Jungle

The jungle, tall trunks blocking
out the blistering sun.
The jungle, hear the animals
make noise and run.
The jungle, the scent of
ripeness from fruit and flowers.
The jungle, darkness under
huge thickened trees.
The jungle, booming a million bees.
The jungle, covered fruit and leaves.
The jungle . . .

Ollie Clements (13)
Bury St Edmunds County Upper School, Bury St Edmunds

I Wish!

Feeling blue,
dreaming of a better life.
I wish I wasn't different.
I wish I wasn't lonely.

Sitting on the street,
With no money and no home.
I wish I had a family.
I wish I had a smile.

I feel like a snowflake on the
Bottom of the ground.
I wish I was as warm as a fire.
I wish I was happy.

I look like an Eskimo.
I'm as cold as ice.
I wish I had a life.
I wish . . .

Amber Warren & Emma Cochrane (13)
Bury St Edmunds County Upper School, Bury St Edmunds

Nativity

The lights were sparkling on the stage,
Music bouncing off the cold, winter brick wall,
As I walked down the centre line
The bright lights reflected on me,
My wings waving at the audience as I walk,
I stood on stage smiling nervously.
We sang, 'Twinkle twinkle little star',
The play was a success
And people really got into the Christmas play,
The Christmas nativity play.

Kim Lumbis (14)
Bury St Edmunds County Upper School, Bury St Edmunds

Dare!

'Go on I dare you!'
'Don't be a scaredy-cat, just do it.'
He slowly picked up the beads which are two small bullets,
One was forest green, the other was jet black,
We egged him on all the way,
He picked the bullets up from the table,
One blink of the eye and he had done it,
They were up!

'Hold on stay still,'
The pepper scratched,
One of the bullets flew out,
It was the forest green bead,
The other bullet wouldn't budge.
We tried and tried,
The pepper kept scratching.
The tissue felt anxious,
We waited and waited,
But no jet black bullet appeared.

'Hmmm,'
Said the doctor with his tweezers held tightly.
Slowly the jet black bullet appeared,
The bullet lay on the table,
The bead was like a cat's eye, shining in the dazzling hospital light.

Katie Mathers (14)
Bury St Edmunds County Upper School, Bury St Edmunds

The Outsider

This person is so sad, sitting next to a lamp,
People kept saying he was a dirty old tramp,
This person is a loner and it's driving him mad,
He is a scrounger he needs money,
Now he just ate a roasted bunny,
He was misunderstood, very outcast,
Couldn't tell the difference, from his own past.

Sam Welham (13)
Bury St Edmunds County Upper School, Bury St Edmunds

Slimy Snake

Slimy snake I'm green and long
And my name's Jake
I can change my colour when I want
I might be green, maybe red
You just don't know when I'm your bed.
So when you're sleeping, keep one eye peeping
Here I am, slimy snake
I'm green and long and my name's Jake.

Josh Turner (13)
Bury St Edmunds County Upper School, Bury St Edmunds

The Outsiders

I sit in my cage
Day after day
The only time people look at me is to laugh
I have no friends
When will this end?
The thing next to me says
'I don't know if I'm red or blue . .
I'm a chameleon.'

Harley Miller (13)
Bury St Edmunds County Upper School, Bury St Edmunds

The Outsiders

I'm sitting in the playground,
All on my own,
I'm hiding from the bully,
The one that's got the phone.

He never used to be so popular,
Only since he got that phone
And now he's got so many friends,
So I'm left all alone.

Amy Manning (13)
Bury St Edmunds County Upper School, Bury St Edmunds

The Outsider

Cold and homeless
The boy walks slowly onwards
The lake shining like the moon

The boy is cold and very lost
He is feeling very sad
The lake still shining like the moon

Suddenly the lake disappears
Making the boy feel even more lonely
So he sits down and settles to sleep.

Andrew Kimpton (13)
Bury St Edmunds County Upper School, Bury St Edmunds

Lightning

The power of lightning
Roars through the air,
People stand and stare.
Trees and animals stand at risk,
By the power of the mighty beast.
After the lightning has gone,
People stand and stare at the destruction
That the beast has done.

Rob Plumb (13)
Bury St Edmunds County Upper School, Bury St Edmunds

Snakes

The snake hisses as it slides through the long pointy grass
Using his forked tongue to sense danger ahead.
His patterns and colours help him blend in the background.
Having scaly yellow and white skin so his predators will think
It's just a colourful scenery and 'snap' goes the snake's mouth
Swallowing its prey whole.

Jonathan Moffat (13)
Bury St Edmunds County Upper School, Bury St Edmunds

The Outsider

A blanket of snow
as white as the clouds
lay on the freezing field.

Boys and girls all around
flinging snowballs, making snowmen.
All apart from one.

The new boy from far away,
was standing there on his own,
too shy to speak,
but so eager to make friends.

He feels like an outcast,
not accepted, lonely, ignored.
He desperately wants his voice to be heard.

Other children don't like him
They're always giving him sharp cold stares
like icicles.

He desperately wants
to break the ice.

Lauren Harker (13)
Bury St Edmunds County Upper School, Bury St Edmunds

The Wind

It's always there
It's all around us
You can't see it
But you can feel it
There when it's sunny
There when it's snowy
You can hear it whistling in the air
It's like the sea in the winter mornings
But nothing can kill the wind
It will always be there till the Earth dies.

Emily Cawston (13)
Bury St Edmunds County Upper School, Bury St Edmunds

The Outsider

Laying on the cold icy floor,
In the middle of winter,
It was like lying on an icy rink.

With nowhere to go,
Not being accepted by anyone
Lying on the floor,
Looking at the bright, shiny stars.
It is like looking at a Christmas tree.

Days go by and by,
People are still running away,
Not letting me buy something
Out of the shops.
It was like a huge pack of animals
Running away from me.

Gemma Manning (13)
Bury St Edmunds County Upper School, Bury St Edmunds

Fish

Here I am a little fishy
Please don't kill me and put me on a dishy
Don't kill me or put me in your frying pan
You nasty horrible big fat fishing man.

Jack Brame (13)
Bury St Edmunds County Upper School, Bury St Edmunds

The Forgotten

On a Monday winter's morning,
There was a blanket of snow.
Upon the snow was a boy,
A boy as lonely as a distant star,
Forgotten like a broken toy.

Hannah Otterson (13)
Bury St Edmunds County Upper School, Bury St Edmunds

Lightning

Dangerous lightning flashes down,
　With some loud thunder.
　　The light flickers like a torch
　　　And scares everyone about.
　　　　It strikes down and hits the trees,
　　So they burn and fall to the ground.
　　Dangerous lightning flickers around,
　With some loud thunder.
　　　The lightning blinks so suddenly,
　　　　It flashes before your eyes.
　　　Dangerous lightning flickers down,
　　　　　With some loud thunder.

Lana Watson (13)
Bury St Edmunds County Upper School, Bury St Edmunds

Thief

As the wind whistled through the trees
It was sun up at dawn
Something moved in the shadows
His wit, sharp as a thorn

As sun rose higher in the sky
It bounded away in leaps
It runs away from anything
Because of what it keeps

With hair as black as night
And eyes of emerald green
With lips as red as rubies
And yellow teeth he can't clean

He robbed the London bank
It started as a dare
He was brave and bold
But now retreats to his lair.

Matthew Greenwell (10)
Fulbrook Middle School, Woburn Sands

Georgia Pulford! (Me)

G orgeous
E xcellent
O utgoing
R andom
G roovy
I ntelligent
A mazing

E nergetic
D aring
I ndependent
E legant

P erfect
U nique
L ively
F unky
O utstanding
R esponsible
D evilish

That's me!

Georgia Pulford (10)
Fulbrook Middle School, Woburn Sands

Autumn

His stare makes leaves turn brown and fall off the trees.
Sometimes he will walk quickly and other times slowly.
With feet that crackle like the crunching of leaves,
There is a gentle wind around him.
This stirs up all the leaves.
His skin is quite soft and can easily be punctured,
It is covered with clothes starting to decay.
There is a mist in the air.
His fingers are gnarled with the autumn chill
And he looks sad because everything is dying.

Timothy Byrne (10)
Fulbrook Middle School, Woburn Sands

What's The Point?

The crane fly has the most deadly poison
Ever known to Man, but no teeth
And only lives for a day
What's the point?

Koala bears with fingerprints
Confused as crimes with humans
What crime would that be?
What is the point?

Elephants swim two miles out to sea
Only to get caught by the coastguard
And get dragged back to shore
What's the point?

The panda's becoming extinct
We can't help it live
It won't even help itself
Does anyone see the point?

Millions of insignificant humans
Get up every day for the same routine
What's the point?

Dan Cause (16)
Greensward College, Hockley

Basketball

B asketball so curved and round
A lley-oop, well timed and class
S kill, timing is everything
K angaroo jumps like a player dunking
E asy going, be relaxed and calm
T eam spirit, hardly ever broken
B alance, the key to passing
A win feels great
L uck, never plays a part in this sport
L anguage, you've got to talk to teammates.

Greg Longman (12)
Greensward College, Hockley

The Caravan Place

The caravan place is the place to come,
Nans and grandads, dads and mums
Sitting in the caravan all day long
At least until the day's all gone.

Fishing lakes all full of carp
Not too tasty, not too sharp
Spiky little perch, one or two cod
Reeling them in hooked on the rod

Pumping music in the club
Children there and adults in the pub
Singing and dancing all night long
But make the most of it, before the last song

Missing people whilst you're away
But we're going home soon, so we'll see them anyway
Writing postcards to family and friends
They might be late, they'll get there in the end.

Emily Higgs & Chloe Graham (12)
Greensward College, Hockley

Because Of The Bully

For this last note I have little time,
From telling the tale to committing the crime,
I am the author of my own fate,
Each of my endings I took time to create,
This is my battle I admit defeat,
Saved by my soldiers I paid my deceit,
Like the last leaf from autumn's fall,
I run, I crawl from this battle called school,
My war, my hell, is that very first bell,
Their army, their fire, from this I tell
Of once walking the perfect paths
Now all I see is paths of glass.
I didn't go down without a fight,
End of Year 11 and I will see the light.

Katey Horrocks (13)
Greensward College, Hockley

All Is Not Fair

Since when is love a crime in small places,
Destroyed by guns and war, horror and hate,
The only crime is horror on faces,
Country to country we were once a mate.
Betrayed by some, hated by many were they,
With no food or water, dying alone,
For only a short time were they to stay,
With a single tear dropping, but no moan,
Do you ever regret something you've done?
People do wrong without even knowing
Some think it's probably a bit of fun,
Like pushing people when it is snowing;
If you don't like who you are no one will,
Leave it to the people, rulers will kill.

Katie Chamberlain (12)
Greensward College, Hockley

The Man From Mars

There was an old man from Mars
Who liked to drive cars
He crashed into a jeep
And collided with some sheep
And ended in a collection of jars.

James Hull (15)
Greensward College, Hockley

Sea

The sea can be many things.
A place of fun and laughter,
A place of calm, peace and relaxation,
A place of beauty and amazement,
A place of excitement and thrill,
A place of death and destruction.

David Edgington (12)
Greensward College, Hockley

Recurring Nightmare

She woke up, nothing was wrong
In the house she'd lived in for so long
While she'd been there nothing had changed
For some people it would seem quite strange
Her mum went out, as usual of course
She closed all the doors which took quite a force
There she was alone again
Sad and lonely, without a friend
She went downstairs with a shudder
Sensing the presence of another
She poured her breakfast into a bowl
She felt someone's breath, it was so cold
She felt a hand on her shoulder
The breath was getting colder and colder
This had given her quite a scare
For her it was all a big nightmare
When she turned around she couldn't believe what was there
A dark face with dead white hair
It was odd, one of a kind
Out of life and lost of mind
Terrifying, scary, such a fright
Holding a razor-sharp knife
Stabbed and stabbed no time to recover
She looked up at the face . . . it was the ghost of her mother
Again and again she had to endure
She could not escape, she could not ignore
Every day over again
Reliving her death, and the betrayal of a friend.

Stephanie Hawkes (12)
Greensward College, Hockley

Emotions

They follow you around
Changing from time to time
Some good and some bad.

Sophie Hand (12)
Greensward College, Hockley

Don't Want To

Can't figure out the reason
I'm the only one to blame
Never thought things would turn out this way
I'm sorry for the tears I made you cry
You caught me off guard

Now it's too late
This time it really is goodbye
The words hit so hard
Can't explain what I'm feeling now
Don't want to conceal this feeling somehow

Nothing is quite the same
Didn't want this fame
Just leave and turn around
Don't come crying back to me.

Hannah Brookes (12)
Greensward College, Hockley

Summer

When the sun is shining right through the day
You know it is that hot, fine time of year
Time to have fun with friends and family
Summer is great, it is the time to cheer
Whether you are relaxing in the sun
Or having a family barbecue
Sports day's in the summer it's time to run
Some don't like summer but only a few
Having fun, water fights in your backyard
While all the adults are just chilling out
When there is lots of heat some find it hard
Summer is loved it's easy to work out
The summer is my favourite season
It's fun and great and that is my reason.

Katie Robinson (12)
Greensward College, Hockley

Environment Poem

Smoke and steam, in our air,
Pure air to breathe, is so rare.
New children to the world, breathe it too,
Everyone suffers, even me, even you.
Nothing is natural, the Earth is being destroyed,
Future generations will be annoyed.

We know we should recycle more,
Everyone thinks it's such a bore.
We should cut down using cars and walk,
But our world does nothing but talk.
Our countries don't consider the poor,
They care about land and money more.

Every day when you hear bad news,
Don't be surprised our world will lose.
So think how lucky you are today,
Remember someone sad far away.
Could we all stop and change it somehow,
Or is it time to give up now?

Georgia Branton (12)
Greensward College, Hockley

My Poem

There's always a group of girls,
who look like a rare type of pear.
With their perfect nails and hair,
make boys jump in the air.

They strut around like they're the best,
think everyone else is the pest.
Heavy make-up
and high shoes
designer label
TV cable
piercings all over
Think they're a four-leaf clover.

Sarah Williams (12)
Greensward College, Hockley

Darkness

The darkness enters, as the day does retire,
It is broken only by light bulbs or fire.
It was once our watch, it was once our time,
We now know it's twelve when the big clock does chime.
We fear it as if it were some kind of sin,
We are too scared to face it and what dwells within.
Darkness has been translated to 'tomb',
For tales of horror are set in the gloom.
We have constructed ourselves little illumination,
Yet dusk remains unbeaten by our measly creation.
Electricity is great for when daylight does dim,
But it is no match for the chief creator of grim.
There would be no fear of the dark that draws in,
Had there not been made such tales of this sin.
We shall continue to cower in our beds and in our room,
For eternity, we shall never rid ourselves of the gloom.

Toby Challis (12)
Greensward College, Hockley

The Flight

We sat in our seats when it started to move,
The aeroplane was going to the runway,
Another passenger needed to be soothed,
Drinks were served and we needed to pay,
The plane was going extremely fast now,
It felt like a fast roller coaster ride,
The aeroplane took off and I said, *'Wow,'*
I was on a window seat on the side,
Now we were getting very, very high,
I was feeling that I was a bird,
On the lunch menu was a lovely pie,
I was sleeping and suddenly I heard,
A thud as we touched down on the hard ground,
Our next flight will be Canada-bound.

Paul Hixson (12)
Greensward College, Hockley

The Water

I dip my toes in the water cool
By the floating flowers
In the sparkling lake
Full of mysterious powers.
Why does it ripple, why does it shine?
The feelings they are just so fine,
As the ripples begin to fade,
I sit under the willow in the lazy shade.
I watch the minnows playing,
It's a beautiful day, a beautiful day,
Let's all watch the minnows play.
I flick back my hair and make a dive,
To play with the otters and their jive.
My dress made of willow leaves,
As tiny as I am,
Flares and floats me
And I flutter my wings as fast as I can
And release myself from the water
And fly home to my beloved daughter.

Olivia Kinsman (12)
Greensward College, Hockley

Little Monkey

Little monkey running through the trees,
Moving faster so no one sees,
His little hand with his cage's keys,
Now he's on the tree, eating honey that belongs to the vicious bees,
Oh now look! There goes his knees,
Ha, ha, ha see how he flees.

Amanda Ince (13)
Greensward College, Hockley

Terrible Teacher

If I had done my homework last night,
I wouldn't be in trouble,
If I had done it straight away,
I wouldn't have to do double.

My teacher has it in for me,
He's hated me since Year 7
And if he had his way he would,
He'd send me to a school in Devon.

He thinks I'm not clever, or brainy, or smart
He teaches me nothing I've lacked,
So every day I try my best,
I try to get him sacked.

Amy Kerrighen (12)
Greensward College, Hockley

What Am I?

I am faster than the fastest sprinter
So powerful I will change your life
Yet the simplest of things will stop me
I crash more times than I can count, going faster than a car
Yet I remain unscathed
I am all around
You see me yet you don't see me
The blind know I exist yet cannot see for themselves
Without it you would not see this riddle
What am I?

James Kent (12)
Greensward College, Hockley

My Picture Poem
(Inspired by the painting 'Home from Sea' by Arthur Hughes)

The day is peaceful but he is not
He seeks it but is forever gone
He has lost something dear
Love
Just laying there like a statue
Waiting if she will come
With loneliness and distress he lays
Realising she really has gone
Above
But the boy is not alone for his love will always
                            be watching over him.

Sadikcha Malla (12)
Greensward College, Hockley

So Unfair!

But Mum she hit me, why do you always pick on me?
It's so unfair!

Mum why would I hit her with a baseball bat?
That's so unfair!

Dad as if I was going to stab her with a pen,
All she ever does is fake and whinge.
It's so unfair!

Why's everyone horrible to me?
It's so unfair!

Sam Kerr (12)
Greensward College, Hockley

A Special World

A special bond one cannot see,
It wraps us up in its cocoon
And holds us fiercely in its womb.

Its fingers spread like fine spun gold,
Gently nestling us to the fold
Like silly threat it holds us tight,
Bonds like this are meant to last.

And if a thread may break,
A new one will form and take its place
To bind us closer and keep us strong,
In a special world, where we belong.

Racheal Barrett (14)
Greensward College, Hockley

Rain

The sky was dark and grey,
When the rain fell down today.
Showering the trees and grass,
Beating against the shiny glass.
Tapping on the window next to me,
Falls the rain so heavily.

Tap, tap, tap it falls to the floor,
Splashing more, more and more.
Flooding everywhere,
Without a care.
The rain, as it fell down today.

Kirsty-Ann Russell (12)
Greensward College, Hockley

Shrek

He is so green
But very nice
Never mean
He didn't kick out the three blind mice

It's Shrek, he's ugly
It's Shrek, he's ugly

He's very large
He has got a big belly
Not associated with Simpson, Marge
He's probably smelly

It's Shrek, he's ugly
It's Shrek, he's ugly

Donkey tried to be his friend
Shrek thought he was funny
Shrek tried to pretend
He's not Shrek's pet bunny

It's Shrek, he's ugly
It's Shrek, he's ugly

Princess Fiona came
Shrek acted like he didn't care
It's such a shame
Pretending doesn't get you anywhere . . .

It's *Shrek,* he is ugly!

Callum Freel (13)
Greensward College, Hockley

Tsunami

The 26th of December,
The sun was shining bright
The tourists didn't know,
They were in for a fright.

The sky grew darker,
The wind blew up high
Everything fell silent,
You couldn't hear a sigh.

People started screaming,
Their voices full of fear,
Shouting for their family,
Who couldn't even hear.

Then the wave took them,
Pulling them away
150,000 lives,
Were lost on Boxing Day.

The day after Christmas,
A thirty foot wave
Came rushing to the beach,
No one could be saved.

Whilst we were talking happily
And playing with our presents
People pulled out bodies,
Whose souls had gone to Heaven.

Money is raised for charity,
For people who lost their love
Providing food and water,
Will never be enough.

Eve Leonard (12)
Greensward College, Hockley

A Class Of Children

The teacher turns her back,
The children mumble,
The children whisper,
The children talk,
The children shout,
The teacher turns back and all is silent.

The teacher turns her back again,
The children are more cautious now,
The back row whisper,
The back row shout,
The next row whisper,
The next row shout,
The teacher turns around again,
She is brighter than they thought.

The teacher turns around for one last time,
The children change their approach now,
Jimmy whispers,
Claire whispers,
Tom whispers,
The teacher is furious now,
That's it, class detention.

Esther Coyte-Broomfield (13)
Greensward College, Hockley

Cars Poem

Big wheels and stereos are the thing to have,
But most people would probably think that you are a Chav.

GTIs and turbos make you very fast,
If you have one of these, you will never come last.

Wheels spinning left, wheels spinning right,
Cruising down the seafront all through the night.

They say not to drink and drive,
It's good there's lucky ones, still alive.

Edward Dale (12)
Greensward College, Hockley

Elemental Sense

Whistling wind,
Chirping birds,
Such a melody,
Never was heard.

Creaking trees,
Twisting vine,
Never a tapestry,
That looked so fine.

Salty oceans,
Fresh smelling seas,
Such a smell,
Does definitely please.

Fine silk thread,
Soft white fur,
Never a touch,
Before has occurred.

Fresh summer cherries,
Picked from the tree,
Such a taste,
Would fill us with glee.

Joe Nash (12)
Greensward College, Hockley

What Am I?

I am circular and smooth,
You can't really feel me,
You can barely see me,
I am glossy and metallic,
There is more than one of me,
I start as a liquid,
Then I fill with air.

I sluggishly float into space before I . . . *pop!*

Christy Hause (12)
Greensward College, Hockley

My Poem

Love is like a cat,
When it pounces there's no stopping it.

It holds you in its embrace,
Cupid's arrow will always hit.

Sometimes it's love at first sight,
Sometimes it takes a while.

But I guarantee that love you'll see,
It'll always make you smile.

Jessica Ridgway (12)
Greensward College, Hockley

Thunderstorm

Lightning strikes
Drum roll thunder
Sending my hair up in spikes
My bed is the one the cat is under

Drum roll thunder
I love it!
My bed's the one the cat is under
My cat hates every little bit

I love it!
The thunderstorm
My cat hates every little bit
Lightning and thunder the sky will adorn

The thunderstorm
It's waiting still
Lightning and thunder the sky will adorn
Now it's lying dormant, waiting to kill

It's waiting still
Sending my hair up in spikes
Now it's lying dormant, waiting to kill
Lightning strikes.

Megan Wisdom (11)
Halesworth Middle School, Halesworth

I Like Cricket

I like to play cricket
I have some cricket wickets
One fine day I won a ticket to see the cricket
And I saw Harmison get a wicket.

I saw some amazing cricket wickets
England played ever so well
Then I saw Flintoff get a wicket
But unfortunately Ponting dived and fell.

But England kept on playing ever so well
Good for England, Vaughn hit a six
But not good for Australia, again Ponting missed and fell
Now Australia were really in a fix.

That was the England and Australia test
Australia scored 250 runs but England scored 253 runs
Of which it was their very best
In the end England got three more runs than them and won.

Angus Mackay (11)
Halesworth Middle School, Halesworth

Moonlight Dream

I had a dream the other night,
About a unicorn in the moonlight,
The moon was glowing through the hills,
But I think I was taking sleeping pills.
The unicorn had a goal,
I think I crashed into a pole.
The unicorn started racing,
The pole looked like it was pacing.
The foal stopped for a drink,
I think the foal was turning pink.
The unicorn went to sleep,
Before I went I took a peep.
Wait now I saw Little Bo Sheep,
Or is it Bo Peep?

Sophie Rudd (11)
Halesworth Middle School, Halesworth

Homework

Homework, homework it's driving me up the wall,
I think I'm starting to bend,
I wish I was tall and not small,
Then the homework would end.

I think I'm starting to bend,
I do a bit in school,
Then the homework would end,
So I've more time to play in the pool.

I do a bit in school,
So I have more time to me,
So I've more time to play in the pool,
Then the weekends are free.

So I have more time to me,
The damage it's done will never mend,
Then the weekends are free,
Especially to me as there is no end.

The damage it's done will never mend,
Over all it does not fit,
Especially to me as there is no end,
It's utter rubbish, every bit.

Over all it does not fit,
Then the homework would end,
It's utter rubbish, every bit,
Homework, homework it's driving me up the wall.

Philip Moyse (11)
Halesworth Middle School, Halesworth

Homework

There's just too much,
I just can't take it, it's such a bore,
It's just like reading Dutch,
The teachers just like giving us more.

I just can't take it, it's such a bore,
Drawing's fun I suppose.
The teachers just like giving us more,
My homework's always full of lows.

Drawing's fun I suppose,
Essays keep me up till ten,
My homework's always full of lows,
If I don't stop soon I'll break this pen.

Essays keep me up till ten,
Pen, pencil, rubber, ruler,
If I don't stop soon I'll break this pen,
Why are teachers such good rulers?

Pen, pencil, rubber, ruler,
Help me now or I'll dissolve,
Why are teachers such good rulers?
This mystery I've got to solve.

Help me now or I'll dissolve,
This homework's really bad,
This mystery I've got to solve,
I think I'm going mad.

This homework's really bad,
It's just like reading Dutch,
I think I'm going mad,
There's just too much!

Kelly-Ann Dilloway (11)
Halesworth Middle School, Halesworth

Snake In The River

S hake the slime off my back
N ever touch or move I do not bite
A nyone who comes near me will go home in one piece
K ind and caring
E ntertaining just not scary

I rritating slithering sound
N ervous around the green grass river

T ongue as long as the river itself
H earing the sound we all run
E veryone looking back as the snake begins to chase

R attlesnakes everywhere
I n I come for my chase
V ery hyper to chase another
E ntering deep river
R attles begin to shiver.

Stephanie Cadle (11)
Halesworth Middle School, Halesworth

My Secret Sunspot

I love to sit on my bench at about five o'clock
Because . . . shall I tell you why? OK then.
The golden sun starts to set with a fiery red background.
It reflects on my pond with the wavy lines
Making it look like I'm dreaming.
I'm not, I know I'm not.
The wildlife whispers, I hear crickets.
The long grass waving in the air
The birds tweeting, they sound like
They're saying goodnight.
What's that? Could it be?
Yes I'm sure it is.
It's the white stag.
Wow.
In my secret sunspot.

Rebecca Bradshaw (11)
Halesworth Middle School, Halesworth

Little Red Squirrel

One blustery autumn day,
where the leaves cover the ground
like a huge orange carpet,
little red squirrel comes
out of his warm cosy home
into the cold breezy woods.

He scampers down
onto the soft ground below him.
Then he spies an acorn.
He scampers over, and picks it up
with his tiny sharp claws.
He stores it in his mouth,
where he won't lose it,
and quickly and quietly
scampers up the bark
and into his cosy home
where he is warm and safe.

Polly Aldous (11)
Halesworth Middle School, Halesworth

Friends

A friend is someone you can trust,
tell them a secret and they will keep it.

A friend is someone who doesn't criticise,
who likes you as you are.

A friend is someone who comforts you
helps you in times of trouble.

A friend is someone honest,
who won't talk behind your back.

A friend is someone you have forever
who will never leave your side.

Amy Woolnough (11)
Halesworth Middle School, Halesworth

Feelings

The best of your efforts are far from the truth,
The best is always to come.
Have faith in your instincts that are placed upon you,
These will guide you to the truth;
Judge as you may but always remember,
To say is not to be.

Never feel sad and never feel bad,
Because the love is always upon you.
The feelings inside you will be the feeling upon you
And these will never leave you.
These can be made but easily pushed away
And if, they will come back to haunt you.

The best of your efforts are far from the truth,
The best is always to give.
Your instincts will tell you if you follow them
When the time is right to give these bundles to others.
These will only guide you to the truth.
If these are given when the time is right,
You will never feel sad or bad.
The feelings inside you will be the feelings beside you
And will never come back to haunt you.

These cannot be taken.
The best is always to give.

Mikey Benjamin Shaw (11)
Halesworth Middle School, Halesworth

Tim!

I am a boy my name is Tim
I come from beyond the rainbow
I feel like I've committed a sin
I wear a halo

I come from beyond the rainbow
I enjoy eating food
I wear a halo
It puts me in a good mood

I enjoy eating food
I like going to the zoo
It puts me in a good mood
I always want to go on the canoe

I enjoy eating food
I feel like I've committed a sin
I always want to go on the canoe
I am a boy my name is Tim.

Tim Macardle (11)
Halesworth Middle School, Halesworth

Sport

Hiking is my favourite sport,
I like biking too.
Tennis makes me bounce a lot,
Swimming's cool to do.

Cricket's OK, I like to bowl,
Football's great when you score a goal,
Rugby's fun when you're in a scrum,
But hiking's still my number one.

Andrew Broadhurst (12)
Halesworth Middle School, Halesworth

Planes

Big, fast, small, slow, jets,
There's ones I cannot tell you about,
Ready to see some, why don't we, let's,
You don't know them all, I doubt.

There's ones I cannot tell you about,
There's civil, military and private ones too,
You don't know them all, I doubt,
You probably know too few, you do.

There's civil, military and private ones too,
There's props as well as jets,
You probably know too few, you do,
I've won some in some bets!

There's props as well as jets,
A pilot's the best job for me,
I've won some in some bets!
A pilot's what I'm going to be.

A pilot's the best job for me,
Ready to see some, why don't we, let's,
A pilot's what I'm going to be,
Big, fast, small, slow, jets!

Ryan Baker (11)
Halesworth Middle School, Halesworth

Cruelty To Animals!

Being hung from a tree
Being beaten to death
I hate it me
What about poor Beth?

Being drowned by a weight
Being hung from a tree
Being shark bait
I hate it me

Being starved to skin and bone
Being drowned by a weight
Being left all alone
Being shark bait

Being darted in the head
Being starved to skin and bone
To be left until dead
Being left all alone

Being hung from a tree
Being darted in the head
I hate it me
To be left until dead.

Erin Read (11)
Halesworth Middle School, Halesworth

Horse Riding

Horse riding is relaxing you fall into a world of your own
Trotting along with no fear at all
Jumping is great especially over cones
For your horsey things go shopping in the mall

Trotting along with no fear at all
Dressing your horse up is just fun
For your horsey things go shopping in the mall
It's lovely doing a gymkhana in the sun

Dressing your horse up is just fun
Get his hay ready for his stable
It's lovely doing a gymkhana in the sun
It's great riding if you can

Get his hay ready for his stable
Getting medals is just great
It's great riding if you're able
It's fun riding with a mate

Getting medals is just great
Jumping is great especially over cones
It's fun riding with a mate
Horse riding is relaxing you fall into a world of your own.

Eleanor Brand (11)
Halesworth Middle School, Halesworth

The Seasons In Walberswick

I love the beach at Walberswick
And these are my few reasons.
My family enjoys their time up there,
Through all of the four seasons.

The sea starts to warm up,
As spring gets underway.
I grab my bucket and spade,
When we go out to play.

A lovely summer's day,
The waves lap on the shore.
The sea smell wafts over me,
As I open the beach hut door.

We see the last of the sunshine,
While the sky stays blue and clear,
We enjoy our time by the sea,
Before winter comes this year.

It's New Year's morning,
The sea is freezing cold.
I dive in and shiver,
As the coldness takes hold.

Harriet Cox (11)
Halesworth Middle School, Halesworth

Chicken

One day my chicken escaped
She's been with me everywhere
I wondered if she had ended up on a plate
Some people say I shouldn't care

She's been with me everywhere
I wonder if she met a terrible fate
Some people say I shouldn't dare
She might have gone to visit the Tate

I wondered if she had met a terrible fate
She disappeared today
She could have gone to visit the Tate
She might have gone a long way

She disappeared today
She might have been turned into a chicken samosa
She might have gone a long way
Or got run over by a motor.

George Farrow-Hawkins (11)
Halesworth Middle School, Halesworth

Horses

I love to ride my horse
She is very fast
She is great of course
She leaves other horses in the past

She is very fast
She will always be my pony
She leaves other horses in the past
If only she was a boy I would call her Tony

She will always be my pony
She loves to be in her stable
If only she was a boy I would call her Tony
Horse riding is fun only if you're capable

She loves being in her stable
She is great of course
Horse riding is fun only if you're capable
I love to ride my horse.

Sophie Mills (11)
Halesworth Middle School, Halesworth

My Dog!

My dog is five years old
He is very active and fun
He keeps me warm when I'm cold
And we play with him in the sun

He is very active and fun
He comes to me when I call
We play with him in the sun
He likes fetching his ball

He comes to me when I call
He is jet-black
He likes fetching his ball
He doesn't ever slack

He is jet-black
We go for long walks
He doesn't ever slack
When he barks he talks.

Leanne Mills (11)
Halesworth Middle School, Halesworth

Dogs

I like dogs.
I turn the TV over when cats appear.
I also like frogs
Because for that species I have no fear.

I turn the TV over when cats appear.
Dogs play forever
Because for that species I have no fear,
But not mice, no, not ever.

Dogs play forever.
I love all sorts of dogs,
But not mice, no, not ever,
The frogs jump on wet logs.

I love all sorts of dogs.
I also like frogs.
The frogs jump on wet logs.
I like dogs.

Jessie Musk (11)
Halesworth Middle School, Halesworth

Squirrel In The Winter

The squirrel dives apprehensively
from one brittle branch to another.
Searching in the trees for its last hope
of getting any acorns for the cold winter ahead.

And as the squirrel scuttles it sees no acorn
for far up the tall oak tree,
but this squirrel will not give up.

The squirrel carries on up the tree,
occasionally slipping on the icy surface
the bitter frost left as it swept past.

But then the squirrel saw something glowing
white in the corner of its eye.
He looked up and there he saw an acorn
topped with snow.

A new sense of hope came over him,
he looked all around and sure enough he saw
a big bunch of other acorns.
He jumped
and he was there.

Michelle Stanborough (11)
Halesworth Middle School, Halesworth

Cruel World!

I can't believe some of the things I see on TV
You would not like any of your pets to be treated this way
It really upsets me
Animals can't speak so they can never have their say
But that is why we have the RSPCA

If you have a pet make sure you'll love it for life
Hooves so long they can't walk and kept in a dirty stable
How would you like it if I stabbed you with a knife
When you buy fur always check the label

Dogs drowned in deep rivers
Rabbits killed so we can wear blusher
Kittens killed for their livers
Dogs killed for their meat mostly in Russia

I have seen a chicken in such a small cage
Trust me you would not like to be an animal these days
Animal cruelty brings me to such a rage
Animals can't speak so they never have their say
But that's why we have the RSPCA.

Alex Reid (11)
Halesworth Middle School, Halesworth

Our Bike Ride

Yesterday was a bright sunny day,
We went for a bike ride, it felt like May.
Down to the beach with the wind in my face,
Puffing and panting but still no pace.

On a bench by the sea, ice cream in hand,
There sat us with our backs to the land.
Suddenly Coastal Voyager flew out,
Above our heads gulls began to shout.

Families were crabbing with interesting bait,
They caught crabs at such a rate.
A small rowing boat fought the tide,
With people, dogs and bikes inside.

On our way back we heard a loud crack,
Off came my brother who had to walk back.
At home after a refreshing cup of tea,
Dad mended the bike and I wrote poetry.

Philippa Doran (11)
Halesworth Middle School, Halesworth

Sunset

As the evening sunset faded,
I watched.

I watched the birds search for food,
The cars moving on the road,
Children playing.

As the evening sunset faded,
I listened.

I listened to the birdsong,
The trees blowing in the breeze,
The duet of people's feet.

As the evening sunset faded,
I thought.

And as I thought
I suddenly noticed something,

It was nearly dark,
All was silent
As night fell.

Kate Skingley (11)
Halesworth Middle School, Halesworth

The Land Of Prince Willy

There was a young prince called Willy,
His best friend was a goat called Billy,
In the palace near to there,
The young princess was so fair,
That Willy loved her more than Billy.
He and Billy went down the river Trim
And in the middle was a troll so dim,
'Give me jewels and gold, our fairy story will unfold.'
'Here,' said the prince, throwing the things in the river,
They swam down the stream, going hither and thither,
The troll followed, so stupid and dim,
That in the end, he fell in!
Willy and Billy went down the path,
To feel a dragon's fiery wrath,
Willy threw his sword, straight and true
And hit the dragon, who said, 'Oh, poo!'
Willy and Billy set down the track
And brought the fair princess, all the way back,
Willy said, 'Quite frankly my dear, I almost died,
But now, you are here!'
They got married and had four kids
And Billy married a girl goat, called Bibbs.

Sophia Wilson (12)
Halesworth Middle School, Halesworth

The Spell
(Based on 'Macbeth')

Eye of fish and toe of dog,
Wool of sheep and tongue of hog.
A scrape of tar in the cauldron,
Don't forget that leopard's chaudron.
Adder's fork and queen bee's sting,
Giraffe's leg and sparrow's wing.
Just remember this little spell
And make sure you don't tell.
*'Double, double toil and trouble,
Fire burn and cauldron bubble.'*
Scale of crocodile, tail of horse,
Witch's hat and wizard's cat.
Of the raven over there,
Drink this potion if you dare.
*'Double, double toil and trouble
Fire burn and cauldron bubble.'*

Jennie Sherington (11)
Halesworth Middle School, Halesworth

Candle Light

Blazing bright,
Shimmering gold.
Fiery red,
Flickering yellow.
Warm and familiar,
Gently swaying,
Soft, burning candle,
Fleeting temptation.
Smoky flame,
With a mind of its own.

Natasha Smith (12)
Holbrook High School, Holbrook

From Good To Bad

I looked outside my windowpane,
And saw some children playing a game.
I listened to their shouting and laughing,
Until their voices were swamped by a passing train.

I went for a walk in the park,
I was out there until it got dark.
Watching the animals and birds,
And hear up high, a singing lark.

I woke up in the night and heard a kafuffle,
Looked out the window and saw a hustle and a bustle.
The crowd moved away to reveal a fight,
And lying on the floor was my good friend Russell.

I spent the night in A&E,
Praying that the doctors could restore his knee,
Hoping that he'll be able to walk again,
Then a doctor came through and said he'd like to see me.

Richard Hudd (13)
Honywood Community Science School, Coggeshall

Coping With Death

Death surrounds.
It's always around,
You'd better not get in its path,
Its vice-like clasp,
Will always last
For the people who feel its wrath.

It sweeps through your soul,
And its only goal
Is to get into people's minds.
But don't let it get to you,
You know you'll get through
Because wherever there's death,
New life you can always find.

Molly Taylor (14)
Honywood Community Science School, Coggeshall

Angel Face

I see an angel
Bright lights dance before my eyes
Wings, unmeasurable, unfold
Blonde hair cascades down with a sheen
White hands spread out, beckoning.

I see an angel
Not the highway I saw before
Gone is the truck hurtling towards me
Silenced is the screeching of metal against metal
Numb is the agonising pain.

I see an angel
I place my hands in hers
She pulls me up and away
She sings to me
I look into her face . . . and smile.

I saw an angel
I now see my love.

Brittany Staples (15)
Honywood Community Science School, Coggeshall

Special Places

The mountain air, stone cold and fresh
The glistening river valley lit by the golden sun
The sandy desert awash with shells
The rocky mountain edges, jagged and sharp
The sharp taste of saltwater quickly washed away
The bronze beaches, clearer than ever.

These places are full of peace
These places are amongst many thoughts
These places are so special
These places are full of tranquillity
These places are the purest they can be
These places are everyone's dream come true.

Lily Mihlenstedt (14)
Honywood Community Science School, Coggeshall

One Girl's Dream

One man's dream
Turned flour into bread,
Trees into paper,
Rock into skyscrapers.
So why can't one girl's dream
Turn hatred into love,
Misery into hope,
Poverty into history
And death into life?
It can.
One girl's dream can
Change the world
For the boy who held his murdered mother,
For the brother that was forced to
Watch his sister being raped.
For the father that kissed his family
Goodbye for the very last time.
So if one girl's dream can do this,
Imagine what a world of dreams can accomplish.
This is my dream.
One girl's dream.

Rowenna Butler (14)
Honywood Community Science School, Coggeshall

Poverty Strikes

It's not fair; life isn't fair
You sit there dressed in glory.
He sits there dressed in pain.
You lie there, stuffed and happy
Whilst he lies there, empty and sad.
Now he stands there, stooped and shamed.
Is that fair? No life is not fair!

Kirsty Mann (14)
Honywood Community Science School, Coggeshall

Horse Chestnut

We are mad, we are bonkers,
At this time of year, we get out our conkers.
People are looking far and wide,
To find a conker that will bring them pride.
The woods are filled with spiky covered trees,
Beware the pointed tips will stick in your knees.
The day is dragging; the school clock is ticking,
The children are impatient to do their picking.
The school bells ring, the children run,
Ready to have so much fun.
Before we fight, the weapon we make,
Is it best to soak or shall we bake?
Drill the hole and thread the string,
If this is a winner, what joy it will bring.
On the twisted string the conker dangles,
One crushing blow destroys and mangles.
The final battle is ready to commence,
Hordes of children watch each side of the fence.
The chestnut harvest has come to an end,
The winner, next year, his title to defend.

Josh Howorth (13)
Honywood Community Science School, Coggeshall

Attack!

'Attack!' I hear, again, again and again,
Another splat of blood I fear, again, again and again,
Running on the battlefield, sword in hand, again, again and again,
Medical remedies on demand, again, again and again.

Men laying everywhere, again, again and again,
Their widows and children have done their share,
                      again, again and again,
Cutting, hacking, slashing, smacking, again, again and again,
Burning, mashing and trashing, again, again and again.

Robert Clark (11)
Honywood Community Science School, Coggeshall

Hope

All around me I sense the world cry.
Free from happiness and love.
Gushing tears and screams of pain.
Hunger, hatred and greed,
Overpowering selfishness,
Intimidation and inadequacy.
All around me I sense the world bleed.
Longing to be nurtured,
Cured for and loved.
Instead, stinging with pain,
Dreams being slashed
As if straight through the heart.
All around me, I sense the world die,
With starvation of love and compassion.
Warmth morphing into evil
And calmness descends.
Free from gentleness,
And eternal peace.
All around me I sense the world laugh,
Crying, bleeding and death is no more.
Where happiness reins,
Free from destruction
And smiles spread like disease.
Love and warmth fill the air,
All around me, I can sense hope.

Becca Clarke (15)
Honywood Community Science School, Coggeshall

Why Me?

As my head smashes the floor again, I cry out
Hoping somebody will hear my prayer.
Salt tears trickle into my fresh cuts,
They sting with agony.

A boot comes slamming into my jaw, I shudder
Wanting somebody to come and save me.
Blood streams down my ruined face,
It soars with pain.

A kick is driven into my side, I scream
Praying somebody will stop it.
Silence presses against me,
It can't stop the pain.

A sharp blow meets my chest, I shout out
Needing somebody to help me.
Pain washes through me,
It reaches my heart.
Why me?

A last blow smacks my head, I'm silent
I have no more energy.
Relief fills my body,
It doesn't reach my heart.
It will happen again tomorrow.

Beatrice Morgan (15)
Honywood Community Science School, Coggeshall

Poetry

Poetry is a delightful thing
It makes you laugh, it makes you sing,
That catchy line you won't forget,
All those stories you have met.

There are lots of poems you can write,
Poems of courage, poems of fights,
Poems of bravery, love and magic,
Poems of events good, bad and tragic.

A poem can get a point across,
It can stop a mighty loss,
It can change the way you think
And help you find that missing link.

So this poem here has taught you that
A poem stops you from writing tat,
Because poems are really fun,
Why not go now and write one?

Jack Ardley (14)
Honywood Community Science School, Coggeshall

We Will Remember

War brings out all of our fears,
War brings most of us victims to tears.
The bombs and guns that fire in the night,
The planes that take off and fly out of sight.

The man and the boys that go off to war,
Sometimes never come back through the front door,
Families have lost loved ones to this cause
And the soldiers' lives are permanently on pause.

Killing and fighting, so many lives lost,
How long will it take us to realise the cost?
We thank those involved for what they have done,
And we will remember them, with the going down of the sun
We will remember.

Rachel Firth (13)
Honywood Community Science School, Coggeshall

Holiday Apprehension

As you swoosh up to the candyfloss clouds
And soar up just like an elegant bird,
You look down at the patchwork fields below
And stare down at the trees becoming pinpricks.
The air hostess gives out cool drinks, tasty food and fun toys.
You see different shaped clouds through the frosting window,
The sun beams at you from above the fluffy clouds.
Then the foreign ground rushes towards us,
The start of our holiday begins!
As you step off the plane the heat hits you,
The dusty warmth enfolds you.
When you get to your holiday home,
You unpack, settle down.
Then you hit the town to explore all the strange shops,
Finally you feel part of this exotic land.

Jenifer Brazier (12)
Honywood Community Science School, Coggeshall

Best Lesson!

It was the best lesson ever
The first of the week
The children didn't say a word
The teacher didn't speak.

The chairs didn't scrape
As everyone walked in slow
Gazing out from misted glass
At a magic world of snow.

Freya Stone (12)
Honywood Community Science School, Coggeshall

Glory Of War

The fires of battle fade away,
Fire and smoke replaced by the light of day,
The echoes of war cease to sound,
Another leader has been crowned.

His title has been won in slaughter and bloodshed,
But the trumpets erase the memories of the dead.
The place of war becomes a pleasant field,
Devoid of the clatter of sword upon shield.

The sword is hung upon the wall,
Until many generations later, comes again the call,
That it be used in anger and fear
To combat once again with the axe and the spear.

Men have died and men have killed,
But the struggle continues still,
Another lord has broken the peace and calm,
Since the victims of the last battle here, long embalmed.

The fight appears to be without an end,
Until all life has been vanquished and spent,
But the bards will still spin tales of love,
Celebrating the glory of war.

Adam Clark (13)
Honywood Community Science School, Coggeshall

Sea Wind

The sea in the trees
And the waving of the leaves,
As the fresh wind blows
The evening tide flows.

The orange autumn leaves
Like a boat on the seas.
Within dark depths of open space,
Flying in a gust of pace.

The finches glitter,
The seagulls barely twitter,
As the whale of the west wind scatters,
The trees, it batters.

The sprays of the leaves fly
As the lumberjack wonders why.
The west wind had such a powerful force,
It doesn't usually come that far off course.

The harbour is a forest,
Where all the trees used to stand,
But now they've been put to better use.
All thanks to the evil sea wind.

James Smee (13)
Honywood Community Science School, Coggeshall

My Dog, Alfie

Although my dog, he may be small,
Is he weak? Not at all!
He's always there when I call,
He's my dog, Alfie.

Plays and jumps, barks with joy,
Fighting with his squeaky toy,
Making noise 'cause he's a boy,
He's my dog, Alfie.

He eats his dinner really fast,
Making sure no time has past.
He only wants his fun to last,
He's my dog, Alfie.

Then the night begins to come,
The day is over, now he's glum.
So he sleeps with a breathing hum,
He's my dog, Alfie.

Ella Neale (13)
Honywood Community Science School, Coggeshall

Darkness

Lost in a world of hatred, no one to help,
Nothing to calm the pain that's inside me,
Tortured, pushed and pulled, body aching,
Body silently longing for help,
Everybody shouting, nobody kind,
Wrenched back and forth by the darkness inside me,
This is a world of darkness, the horrible times,
Keep coming back, no wonder I'm a sin
Leading people astray,
This is a world of darkness, the lost world of the dark age.

Kieran Dixon (11)
Honywood Community Science School, Coggeshall

Stranger

The stars twinkled in his eyes,
As if they held a thousand lies,
His skin so pale,
He could never fail,
To complete his task,
That night with his mask.

He mesmerised my senses,
As he leaned over fences.
He whispered to the night,
As he dodged the light.
Dancing over flowers,
He seemed to have flying powers.

Windows through, he looked,
Making the occupants hooked.
His penetrating stare pierced right through their brains,
Causing unbelievable pain.
Two blinks he has to make,
For the spell to break.

He seemed to look for trouble,
To help people out on the double.
As I watched from my room,
I felt a blood-curdling doom.
The stranger knew him I saw,
And was quick to show me more.

He zoomed up high,
And said with a sigh,
'My job is extremely hard,
And I feel very barred,
One day you will find,
I'm not evil but kind.'

Emma Cooper (13)
Honywood Community Science School, Coggeshall

Lost . . .

Lost in a forest, far from home,
Not supposed to be there and yet I roam,
In for a dare but chased by a dog,
Now all I can hear is the croak of a frog.

The bark of the trees presses in on all sides
And I'm all alone with no one besides
And the evening light is fading fast
And the trees all creak like an old ship's mast.

A crack of a twig and a clink of old keys,
I turn on my heels and tear through the trees.
But the unseen stranger does just the same
As though he is playing a great chasing game.

the keys in his belt, they shake and they rattle,
To me they belong to a huge herd of cattle.
I come to the gates of an old broken house
And nothing seems to live there but maybe a mouse.

The getting away I desire the most
But a doubt is now forming: could he be a ghost?
But I run up the stairs of the old grey house,
Scattering mice and disturbing woodlouse.

Now on the landing and into a room
Old brown sheets crumbling like the shrouds in a tomb,
A creak of a floorboard and then of a stair,
I look onto the landing and no one is there.

Emily Rose Clarke (13)
Honywood Community Science School, Coggeshall

In The Shadows

A man lay in a corner hidden by the sun,
Just hidden, hidden, hidden.
This man just laid, laid, laid.
Staring through the shadows,
Just staring, staring, staring.

Upon his face a long beard grew,
Just growing, growing, growing.
His eyes were grey
And getting greyer with each passing day,
Grey, greyer, greyer with each day.

People walked past this man in the shadows,
Seeing him, just seeing, seeing, seeing.
The people who judged this man,
Who judged, judged, judged.
Did not truly understand the man.

The man lying in the shadows,
Just watched, watched, watched.
While he was judged by passers by,
By no one who truly knew him,
Knew him, knew him, knew him.

The man who lay in the shadows,
Just faded, faded, faded.
Until one day he disappeared,
Disappeared, disappeared, disappeared.
Without anyone truly knowing who he was.

Kayleigh Webb (13)
Honywood Community Science School, Coggeshall

Tree

I remember the time the first bird sang
Sat upon my branches whilst the church bells rang

I remember when blossom clouded my face
Quickly it brought me style and grace

I remember little girls swinging on my branches bare
Whether they hurt me or not, they did not care

All of my leaves fell to the ground
My bright green leaves, all around

I was alone and cold
Bare and bold
All except my skin of bark
I was now dull, dull and dark

I remember a long time ago
When the songbirds sang whilst the sun was aglow
I thought I would probably die soon, once my last ring had grown
Someone out there will plant a seed of their own

Now that I look down on my old land
I would have thought you'd understand
Why I am sad but happy still
That in my space, a root does fill?

Robyn Woodhouse (13)
Honywood Community Science School, Coggeshall

Torn From My Life

Torn from my habitat,
Torn from my life, my home and sent to start anew.
My only comfort locked away behind key and chain,
My friends gone forever.

Where are we going?
I want to go home, my home, the home I know and love.
Neighbours in my mind still waving goodbye,
But now just the leaves waltzing along the road we have left behind.

The rain starts to fall, drop by drop, placing itself on the car,
As we meander down the road.
It is cold outside, yet I am hot.

We arrive at a house, someone else's home and life,
All their memories just torn from four walls within,
Just as mine were.

I get to my bedroom; it is big, but not big enough
to stop me remembering.
I climb into bed, I am tired yet I cannot sleep.
I'm not comfortable; it's just not the same.

It is the same bed but it's not the same house,
Not the same home.

Haydn Horner (13)
Honywood Community Science School, Coggeshall

How Music Changes People's Lives

There are so many types of music,
Using different instruments and styles,
Each person has their own preference,
Shown through their CD piles.

Music is a great influence,
On the way people live and act,
Through their fashion; the way they dress
And the friends they keep in contact.

As they pass and see a new person,
That they have never spotted before,
They will either look straight around
Or keep turning back for more.

Not very often different people meet,
If they don't enjoy the same sound,
But when they come across someone in common,
They know someone of interest has been found.

Most of the time you can tell,
Who likes what style of music,
Through their choice of dress and mannerisms
And the way they choose to speak.

You may call this stereotyping,
But if you go out and wander
And take a look at the different people,
You'll stop to think and ponder.

Katie Drakeford (14)
Honywood Community Science School, Coggeshall

The City Changing Fast

The silver city shone so bright,
The buildings looming in the night.
Their shadows cast,
Though daylight in the past.
The silver city, changing fast.

Car lights zipped,
As things were shipped.
The port, so busy,
While the ships made you dizzy.
The silver sea, changing fast.

Planes flew high
Up into the sky.
Stars like lamps,
The clouds like stamps.
The silver sky, changing fast.

The moon of metal,
Its rays like petals.
Shone down and settled
As the city slept on.
The silver moon, changing fast.

The golden rays hit the floor
The city lit up,
Night, no more.
The people rose,
The moon now froze.
The golden city, changing fast.

Joseph Baynham (13)
Honywood Community Science School, Coggeshall

What Makes Me?

What makes me?
What makes you?
Is it the sea,
That shines so blue?

Is it the sun,
So big and so round
Or is it the ants,
Crawling on the ground?

Is it the birds,
Who might chase mice?
Is it the snow
As cold as ice?

Is it our friends,
Who laugh and play
Or is it time,
Which records every day?

Is it the world
In the vast-black space.
As it spins and twirls,
With every ounce of grace?

But why are we made
Is the big conundrum
And why are we here,
Is another great sum.

I have the answer,
To all of my questions.
It's me that makes me me,
I make my rules and expectations.

Jonathan Siddall (13)
Honywood Community Science School, Coggeshall

The Stream

I was only a child of eight,
Walking through the woods one day
When suddenly I saw something sparkling,
That led my eager mind astray.

I walked over many twigs,
That snapped beneath my feet,
Not really sure about
What sight I might meet.

Then all at once the trees parted,
And I thought it was a dream.
There right in front of my eyes
Was a beautiful little stream.

The banks were like sandy beaches,
With pebbles dotted about,
It had probably been there for hundreds of years,
Of that I had no doubt.

The water of the gentle stream,
Cascaded through the trees,
Leaves fell down from the deep blue sky,
Dancing in the breeze.

Little fish I also saw,
Gliding effortlessly like a plane,
Boatman insects skimmed the surface
Of their perfect domain.

And when I'm feeling sad or alone,
I sometimes have a dream
That I'm still at that special place,
Watching that beautiful little stream.

James Rossington (13)
Honywood Community Science School, Coggeshall

My Knight In Shining Armour

Sitting in the rain,
Watching the leaves brush by,
I can hear the park swings rattling
As the wind comes thrashing past.
I can't feel my fingers
And I can't feel my toes.
My mascara's running down my face
I just hope nobody knows.

But then it suddenly hits me,
I'm here all by myself,
No one to hear me crying,
No one to see my tears,
I'm just sitting here waiting,
Waiting here still,
For my knight in shining armour
To release me from this spell.

I can feel my mobile buzzing,
But I can't bear to look,
After a couple of seconds,
I pull it out just to take a peek,
But before I can accept it,
I feel your warmth as you speak.
Because you are my knight in shining armour
Trying to release me from this spell.

As you come close,
I feel your warmth surround me
And as you hold me tight
You whisper softly, 'Everything will be alright,'
Yes, *you are* my knight in shining armour
And you have released me from this spell.

Grace Ellis
Honywood Community Science School, Coggeshall

The Storm

A thick damp mist creeps along the ground
No living being to be found
The wind picks up, bending the trees
All of the leaves scattered by the breeze
Nothing in sight
Just a bright flash of light
Nothing in sight, just darkness
As the clouds approach, comes an ice-cold spray of water
It seems as though Death may have come to claim the living
Clutching its throat, so nothing is breathing
Suddenly down comes a bolt of light thrown by the gods
Striking a tree like Thor's hammer on anvil
The tree bursts into flames
Singeing the ground
Still not a sound, no one around
The spray becomes a heavy downpour
Each single drop like a bowling ball on my shoulder
As the rain passes over
The wind picks up, stronger and stronger
Branches snap, no more leaves attached
Ground flowing with water
The stream bursts its banks
The wind dies down
Still no living being to be found
The thunder fades away in the distance
The sun rises slowly
A new day dawns
A new beginning
A fresh start.

James Martin (13)
Honywood Community Science School, Coggeshall

Empty

I've walked round empty corners,
I've walked down empty lanes.
Countless times I've seen them,
Now I'm here again.

I've walked down empty corridors,
I've walked through darkened doors,
Each leading to an empty room,
I hoped I'd see no more.

I've walked through empty gardens,
I'll walk through many more.
My life is full of emptiness,
I hoped I'd get rid of before.

My life might be quite empty,
I mayn't have any friends,
But I have imagination,
So at least I can pretend.

And when I'm old or dead and gone,
And everyone's forgotten me,
I'll walk once more down empty roads,
Just like how it used to be.

Elizabeth Beaver (13)
Honywood Community Science School, Coggeshall

Dolphins

D on't you think they are really sweet
O verall they give you a treat
L ook at how they swim so fast
P owerful, no way they are last
H ow they glide is so cool
I f you want you can keep them in a pool
N obody should bully or tease
S o give them a chance, pretty please!

Verity Michie & Roisin Lightbown (11)
Honywood Community Science School, Coggeshall

Happy

Why is no one ever happy?
There's always something wrong,
No one's ever perfect.
When you're sad, the day is so long.

Why not have a smile every day?
You won't have to worry and you
Will have more time to play.
You will be so happy, you will
Fulfil your dreams.
You will never cry with sadness
But will cry happy streams.

Why is no one ever happy?
There's always someone sad.
If you keep your happy thoughts,
You will forget the sentence,
It's all gone bad!

Holly Boag (11)
Honywood Community Science School, Coggeshall

Discrimination

I met this little boy at school
Nearly everyone is really cruel
He comes from somewhere far from here
So his English language isn't clear
He gets called names, pushed and shoved
I hope when he's home, he gets loved
He believes in things different to me
Has different foods for his tea
The teachers do not understand
Neither does the boy, he needs a hand
I wish that I could be his friend
Or have something that I could lend.

Victoria Nash (11)
Honywood Community Science School, Coggeshall

Spirit Child

Cold and lonely,
Sad in bed.
Lying there
Ache in my head.

My bed is the gutter
Of an empty street,
The ache is a hard pain
From my head to my feet.

The bang of my heart,
Is a crash in my brain.
Going ever so slowly,
Day after day.

I struggle to my feet,
Gazing around.
I trip and my eyes,
Meet the hard concrete ground.

I feel my head
And look at my palm,
It's covered in crimson
Blood, I fill with alarm.

I feel like I'm floating,
It's calming yet wild.
I'm certain it's Heaven,
I'm a spirit child.

Becky Drakeford (11)
Honywood Community Science School, Coggeshall

No More Regrets

It filled me with fright and terror,
It filled me with tears and regrets,
The noises startled me senseless,
The sounds made me forget.
I forgot the pain and torture,
I forgot the aching feel.
All I seem to remember is the need for a meal.

As I lay in the cold and wet,
I think of those we lost,
But my thoughts are interrupted by the sergeant, our boss.
We are up for duty, and ready to go and fight.
I will give it my very best
And try with all my might.

That was many years ago,
But still clear in my mind,
It was not the war that scared me,
But the thought I might have died!

Now my life is peaceful,
No more memories to forget,
I'll spend my time being happy.

Not living on regrets!

Emily Eversden (12)
Honywood Community Science School, Coggeshall

Death Rings
(Based on the D-Day landings)

The sergeant shouts an order
A trooper sobs and sighs
In my head I shout with anguish
Whilst all around me, people die.

The pain must be suffered
The deaths must be endured
But why me, I begged to wonder
Why am I stuck on killer shores?

We scramble up the beach
And take incoming fire
Our boats have been destroyed
And circumstances are dire.

Death rings inside my head
I think I'm dead, dead, dead
Death rings inside my head
Inside my head, head, head
Death rings, death rings!

Duncan Mackay (11)
Honywood Community Science School, Coggeshall

Polar Bears

Polar bears I love the most,
Polar bears not gross.
Polar bears look so cuddly,
Polar bears don't like Mondays.

Polar bears like to eat seals,
Polar bears have them for their meals.
Polar bears live in the snow,
That's where Santa goes, 'Ho! Ho! Ho!'

I love polar bears, you may not,
I love polar bears, lots and lots.

Francesca Burleton (11)
Honywood Community Science School, Coggeshall

What Is It?

Smelly pester
Breath tester
Stale waster
Murky quester
What is it?

Bottom blower
Bladder stower
Perfume knower
Awful go-er
What is it?

Gas bomber
Aroma gonner
Stench slumber
Reek snobber
What is it?

Emily Ambrose (11)
Honywood Community Science School, Coggeshall

Rainbow

Red, yellow, blue, pink,
These are the colours
Of the rainbow I think.

Yellow, indigo, violet, red,
'Red is the colour
Of anger,' he said.

Red, indigo, blue, green,
Wear this colour and
You will never be seen.

So if you see a rainbow,
In the sky,
It's a sign that God
Is watching us with a smile.

Miranda Elliott (12)
Honywood Community Science School, Coggeshall

Invisibility

Secondary school stinks,
That's what I think,
I think it is a true disgrace,
Can't you see tears on my face?

Last year I was so tall,
Now I am truly small,
Everyone just looks and stares
And all I can do is just glare.

After, when I'm on the bus,
Everyone makes such a fuss,
All I want is a seat,
But that's too hard to complete.

I never want to go back again,
I feel like I'm in the rain,
But I feel I have no choice
And no opinion or a voice.

Rebecca Wingar (11)
Honywood Community Science School, Coggeshall

Behind Bars

You don't know if you're living,
You don't know if you will survive.
You don't know when every clock ticks,
You don't know if you'll get out alive.
You don't know why you were locked up,
You don't know why you did it anyway.
You don't know why they really don't notice
You don't know why you're getting mad, day after day.
You don't know why life is bugging you,
You don't know why you can't hear any cars.
You don't know why you're in the middle of nowhere.
You don't know why it's you behind bars!

Louise O'Reilly (11)
Honywood Community Science School, Coggeshall

What Would I Be?

If I wasn't me,
Who would I be?
Would I be a cat
Or a dog or a rat?
Would I be a tree
Or a fly or a flea?
Would I be a man
Or a pie or a can?
Would I be a snake
Or a mouse or a lake?
Would I be a pig
Or a cow or a wig?
Who knows what I'd be,
If I was not me,
What would I be?
I don't know
But I'm happy being
Me!

Bryony Butcher (11)
Honywood Community Science School, Coggeshall

A View

I hate pollution,
It's everywhere,
Litter on the street,
Gasses in the air.

Crisp packets on the floor,
Junk mail at your door,
Chocolate wrappers in the lake,
Car fumes so hot you bake.

I hate pollution,
People just don't care.

Kirsten Bradley (11)
Honywood Community Science School, Coggeshall

I Hope You Will Understand

I've determined the past,
    Runs away much too fast
And we can only be left with sad dreams,
    But I do want to know
Why in sun, and in snow,
    Souls stay muddled and hearts fall apart.
A major debate, this one is too late,
    Of this sadness which we are in debt,
The happiness that could be equally shared,
    Many figures have not yet met.
So unlucky to those who are left in the dark;
    There's nothing much that you can miss
Apart from hatred and lies
    And hearts that despise
To love and to care and to kiss.

Alice Tull (15)
Honywood Community Science School, Coggeshall

The Moon

The moon is a crystal ball of fireflies
    caught in the dead of the night.

It is a curved silver sword dropped into the
    darkness of the sea to be forgotten.

The moon is a ball of glowing wool rolling in
    the darkness of your dream.

It is a bunch of flowered snowdrops to
    lighten the darkness of winter.

The moon is the twisting soul from the
    bed of death.

It is a round silver coin buried in
    the earth, not to be recovered for centuries.

Jennifer Irwin (12)
Honywood Community Science School, Coggeshall

Here's A Helping Hand

Take my hand
Don't walk away
I know you don't fully understand
Help them get their life back
And show you care.

Reach out a hand
For everyone
Every child, woman and man
Abuse has got to stop
Full stop.

Take their hand
If that's you
They'll understand what you're going through
Help, care for you
Just speak to them.

It's not your problem, I know
But abuse has got to stop
Full stop.

Katie Watts (12)
Honywood Community Science School, Coggeshall

Clippoty-Clop

Up and down, up and down, Murphy's head goes,
Clippoty-clop, clippoty-clop, he's riding in a show,
Thump the jockey's legs kick,
Flick-flick Murphy's been whipped,
Clippoty-clop, clippoty-clop.

'Canter on' the jockey shouts,
Then pulling the bit on Murphy's mouth,
Bang he falls, wallop, smack,
He falls off Murphy's back,
No more clippoty-clop.

Tiffany King (11)
Honywood Community Science School, Coggeshall

Nameless

My life floats on open seas,
It sinks in high water but drifts with a breeze,

My boat is broken beyond repair,
It can't be fixed but I don't care,

Clouded by my hopes and fears,
My deep seas are never clear,

The boats I ride are peaks of hope;
Sometimes they sink when I can't cope,

When they sink, a part of me will die
And all I can think is how and why?

But soon another comes along
To fix my heart and right my wrongs.

And when that sinks I'll go to mourn,
But there is always a new dawn.

The ropes get untied so there's nowhere to run,
When a new boat is here, a new story has begun.

It all starts off going just fine,
The weather is good, the current's divine.

But something happens, it all goes wrong,
The sails have ripped, the paddles are gone.

You wonder why you chose this boat,
You wonder if it'll stay afloat.

A final fold and you're over the side
This dream is over, this boat has died.

But soon another comes along,
To fix your heart and right your wrongs.

It's all over, you go back alone
To your boat, a broken home.

Becca Warder (15)
Honywood Community Science School, Coggeshall

Our World, Our Mess

This mess we live in
A foul but no game
Suffocated by air
Whipped by a cane
We're blanketed for life
A war for eternity
We need to end this long-lasting strife.

The Devil in disguise
Stands proud and titters
Watching disgrace
His heart so bitter
He's caught us now
Like a fish in a net
He's got us now, I'll say, you bet.

People passing on too early
Too many fish are eaten,
The Devil stands so big and burly
Never to be defeated.

And so the clouds continue to open
To let the herds pass through.

This mess we live in
A foul but no game
Suffocated by air
Whipped by a cane
We're blanketed for life
A war for eternity.

We need to end this long-lasting strife,
Sans war,
Sans worry,
Sans life.

Harriet Moore (14)
Honywood Community Science School, Coggeshall

Time ...

Time is something we cannot change
Something we cannot rearrange
But ... time is as long as we want it to be
I can make it suit me.

Time comes in many forms
And can be found in many devices
Time is found in many places
Mostly found on clock faces.

Time is fast and slow
Time is short and long
Daytime and night-time
Seconds and minutes.

Breakfast time
Lunchtime
Dinner time
Home time.

Our lives are made of time
Time will always be a mystery.

Ben O'Connell (12)
Honywood Community Science School, Coggeshall

A Soldier's Sorrow

See the man fighting in the trenches,
In his arm is a gun that he clenches,
When he shoots he turns away,
He is really trying to keep his tears at bay,
As it starts to pour with rain,
He looks over no-man's-land, looking in vain.

As he looks at the other deceased men,
He closes his eyes and counts to ten,
He dreams of home and family,
Then he remembers that he must face the cruel reality,
A glistening tear rolls down from his eye,
As he looks up into the bomb ridden sky.

His life has fallen right apart,
He remembers his old horse that used to pull his cart
And how he used to work each day,
Even though he didn't get much pay,
But he is sure that he would prefer,
To work every day instead of saying 'Yes Sir'.

Emily Mathias
Honywood Community Science School, Coggeshall

London's Burning

Commuters head for the Underground
Just another weekday
But what happened later on sounds unbelievable to say
For soon aroused a terrible sound.

A series of explosions on rush hour trains
Fires on the tube, billows of smoke
A putrid, noxious smell that caused commuters to choke
Screams of agony, people shouting at their pains.

Deep underground in those hellish spaces
Rescuers come, finding people who groan
Some survivor with harrowing pictures on his phone
At the hospital people have bewildered faces.

Can we still call this just another week day,
With a capital mourning the people from all over the nation
We hope never to be in this horrific situation
The horror in July was on just another weekday.

Mark McFadden
Honywood Community Science School, Coggeshall

The Game

The clock is ticking, the countdown begins
My legs feel like jelly as I rub my shins
My stomach is churning with all the worry
Let's hope we don't leave in a hurry.

The roar of the crowd is just so loud
I hope the team can do them proud
The chants I hear means they are near
When suddenly there's a great big cheer.

The stamping of feet means we're ready to greet
I can see the pitch, we're in for a treat
Everyone's rushing and pushing past
This sure has started a bit too fast.

The whistle blows for the game to begin
The crowd use this as a sign to sing
As the ball is kicked the tension rises
Let's hope I score and win all the prizes.

Hayden Mihlenstedt (12)
Honywood Community Science School, Coggeshall

My Special Friend

I have found a special friend
The bond I can't explain
She's always there to comfort me
And take away the pain.

She never seems to judge me
She shares in all my dreams
I never have to say the words
She knows just what I mean.

She knows my every weakness
And the problems I've been dealt
She was there for all the bad times
And knew exactly how I felt.

Only now I realise
I've just began to see
That person's in the mirror
She's looking back. It's *me!*

Katie Gardner
Honywood Community Science School, Coggeshall

Fright Night!

Hallowe'en is upon us,
With the witches at their cauldrons, casting spells,
People go missing and end up where evil dwells.

Zombies arise in the night,
Some villagers have died of fright.

Vampires have come for a bite
On this Monday night.

Who is the queen of Hallowe'en
Frankenstein's bride,
She will get you, you can't hide.

Frankenstein's here,
The villagers scream in fear.

Elizabeth Anderson (13)
Honywood Community Science School, Coggeshall

Beachcombing

One day I strode along the shore,
Amongst the stones and shells I saw ...
Some sea glass clear, some sea glass green,
The brightest blue I'd ever seen.

One day, I strode along the shore,
Amongst the stones and shells I saw ...
A lucky stone with holes right through,
Snuggled right beside my shoe.

One day I strode along the shore,
Amongst the stones and shells I saw ...
There on the sand was a shark's tooth,
Twelve million years old, and that's the truth.

One day, I strode along the shore,
Amongst the stones and shells I saw ...
I couldn't believe my sight,
Guess what? It was an ammonite!

Daniel Page (12)
Honywood Community Science School, Coggeshall

The Shadow

A shadow is a creature in the dark that tries to be like you,
A shadow is ever stalking, ever gawking
It copies everything you do.

A shadow will not leave your side whenever there is light
Whenever you're walking, whilst you're talking
It only goes at night.

A shadow follows in your footsteps wherever you may go
It will share your plights and all your fights
But you won't always know.

A shadow has no face of its own
But within you it has its home
It's your eternal friend and will stay with you until the end.

Ross Baker (13)
Honywood Community Science School, Coggeshall

A Day Of Poetry

Standing tall all on its own,
Baying in the wind,
The willow tree is crying,
Its branches drooping down
And all around its single leg
Are many golden leaves.

Nearby the frog, he croaks
And the fly evades his ever watchful eye.
The fish dive and swim and float,
Beneath their water world,
I see a larvae in the pond and wonder what he'll be,
A dragonfly perhaps, like the one upon the reed.

It's evening now, the night awaits;
The bats are flying down,
Skimming the pond, to catch the bugs,
The night is close now,
I hear an owl calling in the dark,
To a partner in the willow tree.

Harry Sparkes (12)
Honywood Community Science School, Coggeshall

People

People come in different shapes and sizes,
They can hide themselves in unusual disguises.
Sarah is tall and slim with long, blonde hair
She is kind and helpful everywhere,
Rocelle has shiny, black hair and smiles a lot,
Wayne always asks 'Why?' and sometimes 'What?'
Chris C likes drawing trains and is good at writing,
All the boys whistle at Amy who loves to dance and sing,
Chris R is strong and broad with lots of sisters and brothers,
Steven is full of charm and loves to amuse others,
With dark, curly hair our Charlton supporter is Abbey,
Michael sings all day because he is so happy,
Mark is a tall, big guy who likes to shout.
At Lancaster School we go out and about,
We go to the gym, shopping and the swimming pool,
We are all different people but we're all very cool!

Amy Mallandain, Christopher Reeves (14), Steven Holiday, Michael Kinsalla (15), Sarah Wingate (16), Wayne Clements, Mark Scott (17), Christopher Coates, Rocelle Vinluan (18) & Abbey Barton (19)
Lancaster School, Westcliff-on-Sea

An Account From Africa

Death,
It's a frightening thought
When no one is there for you
To give you food
To help you when you're down
I work hard every day,
For only fifty pence.

I'm missing school; it's just too expensive
I can only afford to go once a month.
The tsunami didn't help
Thousands are dead,
There isn't enough food and water for everyone.
But our lives have to end sometime but when?

Death,
I'm not afraid
It has to happen sometime,
Weeks,
Months,
Or if you're lucky years.
But now I must go,
Adieu, Adieu …
Adieu.

Zoë Davis (15)
Manor School & Sports College, Raunds

In My Fantasy Wonderland

In my fantasy wonderland
I sit and dream all day
Sitting on the lovely sand
In the middle of May.

I always want to be alone
For I am very sad
But now I hear a lovely tone
And now I'm really glad.

Now I jump around
And bounce along
Hear a sound
And sing a song.

My heart is filled with lovely joy
In this lovely place
Playing with a toy
And having a race.

I came first
Kate came fourth
As my body filled with thirst
We started walking heading north.

Megan Duggan-Jones (14)
Manor School & Sports College, Raunds

The Cupboard

I'm scared of the cupboard,
Under the stairs,
My big brother tells me,
Of what it bares.

'A great monster,
With really loud roars,
Horrid horns
And massive claws!'

'Is it true dear brother?'
I will always say,
'I don't know,
I've never looked anyway.'

So I took one peep,
Behind the door
And as soon as I saw it,
I fell to the floor.

Hayley Coen (12)
Presdales School, Ware

Thunder And Lightning

Her hair is black,
Her eyes are green
And for some reason she is never seen.

Her voice is loud and fills the night,
Which gives little children a terrible fright.

Her friend Lightning stands by her side,
As Thunder does her best to hide.

Lightning flashes and glows in the sky,
As Thunder dances and shouts up high.

Then morning comes as they disappear,
Which gives the world a little cheer.

Ellie Parrott (11)
Presdales School, Ware

7 Stages Of Teddy

Monday, he is just thread,
A piece of string without a bed.

Tuesday, he is shoved in a crate,
Put on a shelf, looking ornate.

Wednesday, a small child full of care,
Chose to love this little bear.

Thursday, going to sleep at night,
With child holding teddy tight.

Friday, no child is there,
College has come, gone is bear.

Saturday, in a garage he stays,
Where he lies alone day after day.

Sunday, no one there to mourn,
When they find poor teddy dead in the dawn.

Bryony Ball (11)
Presdales School, Ware

At A Glance

The future of a tomb,
From a glance across the room,
Love at first sight,
Both dressed in moonlight,
His view on her starts to shimmer
And her moonlight eyes glimmer,
They head to each other from across the room,
As they get closer their love begins to bloom,
Something not to miss,
Was when they shared love's first kiss,
Each one had a love-filled heart,
Even when the time came to depart,
The obstacles they could not see,
But obstacles showed if it was meant to be.

Lucinda Green (14)
Presdales School, Ware

Untitled
(Based on 'To Kill a Mocking Bird' by Harper Lee)

On the doors of closed ears my plea knocked
On the eyes of the blind my evidence faded
On the shoulders of the innocent they threw his guilt
And in the drops of my blood those with hearts drew the truth.

In the open hands of my wife some laid mercy
Whilst beneath the eyes of God others walk past my children
So like the brave - to high walls and closed doors I reached freedom.

Not to Maycomb

On the open doors of Heaven my truth was told
On the open eyes of equality my truth was seen
On the shoulders of the guilty my burden fell
In the house of God
From drops of my blood they found truth.

Luci Surridge & Rebecca Rasheed (15)
Presdales School, Ware

Falling Asleep

The lights were dim,
I heard a slight cough,
Falling asleep,
Waking up every now and then,
Curled up on the soft settee.
Next to me a steaming cup of tea
And a plate of biscuits,
Looking out the frosty window,
Seeing the fog.
I sit closer to my soft toy dog,
The quiet TV light flickered, casting
Long, sleepy shadows,
Welcoming me to sleep,
Asleep in a warm, cosy heap.

Natasha Burns (13)
Presdales School, Ware

Your Common Preconception

You sit with the flock, you look and you frown,
Scared of what may turn your world upside down,
I see you have morals,
You hold them like guns,
Ready to pass down to daughters and sons.
Your fear and your ignorance, they make you blind,
In a world of perfection there's nothing to find.
Difference divides us from one and from two,
Naivety causes a world made of yous.
And what is colour but shadow and light,
Who makes the choice of which colour is right?
And even when skin is so small a part,
How can you compare it to mind and to heart?
To intelligence, courage, bravery and thought,
The heart of the man who was licked but still fought.
The mind of a lady who knew she was right,
Who didn't give up just for fear of the fight.
How brave is the bird who never will fly,
But tries even though it knows it will die.
How can you judge these with ready made eyes,
These cannot be measured by shape or by size.
You are not God, you can't choose who to smite,
I know where my soul lies, I know I am right.

Becky Buttall (15)
Presdales School, Ware

Life Is A ...

Photos, holidays, family and friends,
In life you go round a lot of bends,
Memories, money, chocolate and places,
As you grow through life you see a lot of faces.

Possessions, pets, holidays and fears,
Moods, tantrums, tempers and tears,
Illness, disease, torture and death,
In the last moments of life, you take your last breath.

Keri Gilbert (13)
Presdales School, Ware

Just Think

Polar bears rule the ice caps,
But for how much longer?

Cars, factories and other types of transport
All give off pollution and unwanted gases
This causes global warming
And many animals are losing their homes all because of this.
The main animals are the polar bears in the Arctic region
Their icy floors are melting
Their chilly waters are spreading
No way to get food and nowhere to sleep.

To save these amazing animals
All we have to do
Is recycle paper and use cars less
And you could spare their life
And clear up this mess
So when you throw your paper away think what a
Difference it would make if you recycle.

Alexandra Smith (12)
Presdales School, Ware

Parrot

Copies every word you say,
Chants every single day.

Listens thoroughly on your words,
Picks a phrase to rhyme with birds.

Locked in a cage every day for a week,
Doing nothing but giving cheek.

Eats its food and goes to bed,
Repeating every word you said.

Wakes up each and every morning,
As its presence wakes our dawning.

Emily Phillips (11)
Presdales School, Ware

The Meeting

More people arriving,
the room getting crowded.
The firelit room
illuminates the faces.
Masks glitter in the moonlight;
deep reds, bright golds.
Sequins decorate the masks,
different shapes
for different shaped faces.
The chatter gets louder
and the laughter begins.
The musicians start,
the music fills the room;
Energetic and bubbly.
It signifies to the guests
to seek a partner.
They dance all night,
enjoying the atmosphere.
Two strangers
dance around the room.
Suddenly they meet
at the side of the room,
staring into each other's eyes.
They speak in prose
until there is silence.
A kiss between the two.
They had given their hearts away;
to each other.
Then they leave each other.
Juliet Capulet,
Romeo Montague.
Their parents are arch enemies,
but will their love
bury the ancient quarrel?

Rebecca Hankin (14)
Presdales School, Ware

Romeo And Juliet Poem

Walking through the Capulets' ball;
I see the most handsome young man of all,
With brown hair, thin figure and quite tall.
Cautiously I look around to see if anyone's looking.
No, the coast is clear.
Everyone is drinking and dancing merrily.

I stare at him with excitement;
It's not Paris, who could it be?
Checking my hair and clothes,
I'll wander over I suppose.
Do I look OK? Will he like me?

He's watching me with his bright blue eyes!
I get halfway,
It's mother, I have to look busy.
She blocks my view,
Where's he gone?

I can't see him anymore!
Maybe he likes someone else.
I wait, speechless, until …
He walks over from the side of me.

'May I have this dance?' He spoke softly.
Without answering, I fell into his arms.
What if my father saw me, with him?

The song ended,
He led me to the side.

'You're beautiful,' he whispered to me,
'What's your name?'
'Juliet Capulet,' I answered, 'Yours?'
'Romeo Montague!' he replied.

Laura Page (14)
Presdales School, Ware

Christmas Time Has Come

It's getting colder, outside my door,
Used to be warm, but it is no more.
The leaves on the trees have all turned brown,
The children's faces are fixed in a frown,
Thinking 'bout their days frolicking in the sun,
And when they went to the park and had hours of fun.
Now they're indoors all day,
Nothing to do and nothing to play.
They miss their friends, they miss their school,
They miss swimming in their ice-cold pool.
They can't ride their bikes and stay out late,
That is one thing they dearly hate.
They loved to play in the grounds,
To roll and tumble with their hounds.
But now the leaves cover all of the grass,
The autumn has decided to pass.
Snow is falling everywhere,
People sleigh ride, without a care,
Christmas is only days away,
Delicious mince pies, warm and waiting on a tray,
The tree is up, the present's bought,
Those gifts are eagerly being sought,
By excited children, they can't wait,
For Christmas dinner, on their plate,
The whole family together, there is not one foe,
With couples kissing happily under the mistletoe,
Enjoying all their time together,
Opening their gifts with pleasure,
In the background carol-singers hum,
At last, Christmas time has come!

Bianca Hill (11)
Presdales School, Ware

Love's True State

If you will be my Romeo
and show me through and through;
then I will be your Juliet
and reveal my heart as true.

As I stand with you under the night,
the moon, the sky and stars
I lean against you, hold you tight
our love will guide us far.

As I see you from my window,
your face lights up the sky.
Without you I'd be so low,
if you weren't here I'd die.

How can our love not be told -
our marriage cannot be in dark.
It is my wish for us to be bold,
we will make the angels sing, hark.

We will run away from all the hate,
to bond together in harmony;
Get married in love's true state
star-crossed lovers, you and me.

Kate Hinckley (14)
Presdales School, Ware

Life Is ...

Life is a box of chocolates, you never
Know what you're going to get.
Life is a haircut, you decide how it is
Going to turn out.
Life is like shopping, you don't know what
You're going to buy.
Life is like a film, you don't know how it will end,
Life is like a house, you don't know who will enter next.

Alice Phillips (13)
Presdales School, Ware

The Griffin

Standing beneath the trees so clean,
A beautiful griffin has just been seen.

Standing there under the stars,
You wouldn't believe it is so far from Mars,
For the griffin comes from Mars it does,
While you're thinking, all you hear is a buzz,
Buzz, buzz of bees flying round the head
Of the griffin beautiful, alive but dead,
For it is extinct, I am sad to say
For the griffin's time is up so now it has sadly passed away,
The things we see under the trees,
The griffin, the griffin, the bees, the bees,
They're all just memories of the griffin so sad,
It makes us feel just so bad,
We killed it off, the bumblebees say,
We killed it off in the month of May.
So bad, so bad, so sad, so sad.
'We killed it off, we killed it off,'
We say, the people say.

Beatrice Smith (12)
Presdales School, Ware

Shimmering Beauty

When I display my tail
Feathers shimmer,
Can you imagine what else makes me a winner?
I dance around on my three-toed feet
And prance in a peacock fleet.
No other creature is like me,
I'm on top like the queen bee.
Think of me as I flutter
And set off the foxes in a clutter.
Wish upon a star and here I am and there you are,
I'm the peacock star!

Selma Michli (11)
Presdales School, Ware

Life

Life is a box of puzzles,
You put the bits together.
Some puzzles may be hard,
Like death, divorce and depression.

Life is a box of chocolates,
Some nice, some bad.
Don't eat them too fast,
Save them for longer.

Life is a roller coaster,
You have ups and downs.
You should try it
And enjoy it.

Life is an ice cream
White with black bits.
It could melt away
So savour every bit.

Life is like a path,
It could be smooth or rocky.
You could get lost
But in the end it all ends up in the same place.

Antonia Kitt (13)
Presdales School, Ware

What Is It?

The almighty holder, the creator,
It contains endless fun, love and scare
How can this be?
What creature can be so amazing?
Words wrapped around it, tightly pulling in
Letters digging into its skin,
The love affair,
The almighty scare
What is it?
A book.

Amelia Hicks (12)
Presdales School, Ware

Little Me!
(Dedicated to my sister Mya Patrice Robertson)

A shining star was born today
Her name is Mya, she is my sister,
How annoying I thought she would be,
But she is the closest thing to me,
Her little feet,
Her little hands,
The day she learnt to talk,
The day she learnt to walk,
Watching her grow,
O' how I know,
I love her so,
My little sister,
Remember I'm always here for you,
And I love you too.

Jessica Robertson (12)
Presdales School, Ware

Looking Through My Window

As I look through my window in the morning,
I sit and watch the sunrise,
Turning from red, to orange, to yellow,
I watch the sparrows dancing across the fresh green grass,
I see blackbirds, singing in their nests of twigs and hay.

As I look through my window at midday,
I see my mum, hanging the washing out on the line,
I watch my brother playing football with my dog,
Jumping around and rolling in the mud,
I see my guinea pigs nibbling blades of grass.

As I look through my window in the evening,
I see stillness and calmness as the sun is setting,
I watch, as the stars appear from their hiding place
And I see the moon shining, replacing the sun for the night.

Emma Davies (11)
Presdales School, Ware

Drama Queen

She doesn't have a best bud,
For the drama queen exaggerates too much,
She will argue all day long,
So no one dares to keep in touch.

If she wants something really badly
And in the end she doesn't get it,
She will throw the biggest tantrum,
You will certainly regret it.

While others blend into the background,
She prefers to make a scene,
She's a gorgeous, glowing, tantrum-throwing,
Darling drama queen!

Olivia Mendez (11)
Prittlewell Technology College, Westcliff-on-Sea

War

The war continues everywhere,
The slaughter has begun,
Shooting here and shooting there,
You hate it, but your only option is to run.

The slaughter has begun,
Bullets punch holes all around you,
You hate it, but your only option is to run
You don't want to do it but you have to.

Bullets punch holes all around you,
Run! Run! You must run!
You don't want to do it but you have to.
It is never good fun.

Run! Run! You must run!
Shooting here and shooting there,
It is never good fun,
The war continues everywhere.

John Butcher (14)
Royal Latin School, Buckingham

Mass Murder

Remember the prisoners in the quarry,
Standing in line,
Waiting to see what their future will bring,
Wondering whether they will survive.

Standing in line,
Facing the water's edge,
Wondering whether they will survive,
28 people blindfolded.

Facing the water's edge,
Listening for any sounds facing their death,
28 people blindfolded,
Wishing they could be somewhere else.

Listening to any sounds facing their death,
Trembling, wishing, wanting, trembling with fear,
Wishing they could be somewhere else,
Wishing they could be anywhere but here.

Trembling, wishing, wanting, trembling with fear,
Their last breathing moments alive,
Wishing they could be anywhere but here,
Several rounds with the machine gun . . . dead!

Their last breathing moments alive,
Waiting to see what their future will bring,
Several rounds with the machine gun . . . dead!
Remember the prisoners in the quarry.

Leah Woodford (14)
Royal Latin School, Buckingham

Justice

Who wants their names?
Who cares for their families?
What does it matter about their past,
When they are a threat?

> Who cares for their families?
> The ones who cry are scared and miss them
> When they are a threat
> To the ones who beat, hurt and kill.

The ones who cry are scared and miss them,
There is nothing to be done,
To the ones who beat, hurt and kill,
Judgement Day will come.

> There is nothing to be done,
> What does it matter about their past?
> Judgement Day will come,
> Who wants their names?

Natalija Carlsson (13)
Royal Latin School, Buckingham

Execution

Silence grips all,
They turn to face the water.
Emotionless faces,
Scared to death.

They turn to face the water,
Shouted at, replying with silence.
Scared to death,
Knowing their fate.

Shouted at, replying with silence,
Threatened at gunpoint.
Knowing their fate,
Facing the water.

Threatened at gunpoint,
Emotionless faces,
Facing the water.
Silence grips all.

Joe Lalor (13)
Royal Latin School, Buckingham

Heartbeat

Ba-dum, ba-dum, ba-dum
My heart is going overdrive
Ba-dum, ba-dum, ba-dum
My fate is sealed

My heart is going overdrive
What can I say to describe this feeling?
My fate is sealed
Closer and closer to my death.

What can I say to describe this feeling?
Lining up from oldest to youngest
Closer and closer to my death
I'm knocking at Death's door

Lining up from oldest to youngest
Memories of me as a child doing the same
I'm knocking at Death's door
And I can't run away. *Ba-dum, ba-dum* . . .

Olivia MacLellan (13)
Royal Latin School, Buckingham

The Stranger And The Twins

He and them: the stranger and the twins,
United together; united forever.
Working to save Chile from sins,
Together forever, whatever the weather.

United together; united forever,
Voluntarily bound together with pride.
Together forever, whatever the weather,
Walking in equal, synchronised strides.

Voluntarily bound together with pride,
The invisible handcuffs, imprisoning them.
Working in equal, synchronised strides,
The confident woman, the two brave men.

The invisible handcuffs, imprisoning them,
Working to save Chile from sins.
The confident woman, the two brave men,
He and them: the stranger and the twins.

Chloe Thomson (13)
Royal Latin School, Buckingham

Execution

Soldiers stand with icy glares,
As a prisoner hits the ground,
He lifts his head and pleads for help,
But mercy is not found.

As a prisoner hits the ground,
Another man has died,
But mercy is not found,
Where nothing is allowed.

Another man has died,
A soldier gives a smile,
Where nothing is allowed,
Santiago's secret.

A soldier gives a smile,
He lifts his head and pleads for help,
Santiago's secret,
Soldiers stand with icy glares.

Aidan Cooper (13)
Royal Latin School, Buckingham

The Puppet Show Plot

They will get out of this all right,
People's hands jerking,
The puppeteers' mouths shut tight,
The secret plan is working.

People's hands jerking,
Money thrown onto the street,
The secret plan is working,
The key part of the plan complete.

Many thrown onto the street,
Policemen closing in on the show,
The key part of the plan complete,
Into the van they must go.

Policemen closing in on the show,
The puppeteers' mouths shut tight,
Into the van they must go,
They will get out of this all right.

Laura Jones (13)
Royal Latin School, Buckingham

Execution

Three soldiers firing from their hip
To where unsuspecting prisoners stand
The bullets and the sound does rip
Through this empty and secluded land.

To where unsuspecting prisoners stand
Their faces of horror still painted there
Through this empty and secluded land
They fell as the bullets hit without a care.

Their faces of horror still painted there
The lives taken in a single second
They fell as the bullets hit without a care
An unreasonable death without God's beckon.

The lives taken in a single second
They had their last glimpse of the setting sun
An unreasonable death without God's beckon
Thirty dead men and the deed is done.

They had their last glimpse of the setting sun
The bullets and the sound does rip
Thirty dead men and the deed is done
Three soldiers firing from their hip.

Lauren Garner (13)
Royal Latin School, Buckingham

Unfair Death

The Junta's regime; evil and unfair
The silence of death hangs in the air
They punish and torture within their lairs
A reign of cruelty, beatings and despair

The silence of death hangs in the air
The prisoners facing water, standing terrified in line
A reign of cruelty, beatings and despair
A machine gun stutter ends their time

The prisoners facing water, standing terrified in line
They knew their fate as soon as they spoke out
A machine gun stutter ends their time
Before the bullets hit them, they ushered a defying shout

They knew their fate as soon as they spoke out
The prisoners prayed that justice will prevail
Before the bullets hit them they ushered a defying shout
The innocent captives' corpses hit the water, ghostly pale

The prisoners prayed that justice will prevail
They punish and torture within their lairs
The innocent captives' corpses hit the water, ghostly pale
The Junta's regime; evil and unfair.

Tomas Goodgame (13)
Royal Latin School, Buckingham

Isa's Kiss

Isa's kiss
So exciting
Andres wants more
What next?

So exciting
In the dark
What next?
A relationship?

In the dark
There was a kiss
Start of relationship
What's Andres thinking of?

There was a kiss
In the dark
What's Andres thinking of?
Isa's kiss.

Amardeep Bahra (13)
Royal Latin School, Buckingham

The House Of Laughter

The house of laughter,
not so fun,
to be chained and tortured,
one by one.

Not so fun,
the guns are aimed,
one by one,
they find their graves.

The guns are aimed,
the bullets taken,
they find their graves,
the ground is shaken.

The bullets taken,
there's something wrong,
the ground is shaken,
slaughterers gone.

There's something wrong,
to be chained and tortured,
slaughterers gone,
the house of laughter.

Jenny Raley (13)
Royal Latin School, Buckingham

Execution

There they stand in a row
Backs straight
Like toy soldiers lined up for battle
Backs straight

Backs straight
Standing proud no matter what
Backs straight
Standing praying

Standing proud no matter what
Straight backs
Standing praying
Straight backs

Straight backs
28 people each with a name
Straight backs
28 people down on the ground

28 people each with a name
Here one minute
28 people down on the ground
The next minute gone

Here one minute
Toy soldiers lost in battle
The next minute gone
There they stood in a row.

Vanessa Charman (13)
Royal Latin School, Buckingham

A Silent Quarry

A silent quarry - the peace is disturbed,
Army trucks arrive from the forest
Smoke flying up after them -
They stop.

Army trucks arrive from the forest,
Doing their job -
They stop,
The prisoners at gunpoint.

Doing their job,
The soldiers with their weapons.
The prisoners at gunpoint,
They are lined up by the pool.

The soldiers with their weapons -
They open fire,
The prisoners are lined up, face down in the pool
So many lives, extinguished.

They open fire
The media, with their barrage of words,
'So many lives extinguished,'
They cry.

The media with their barrage of words,
Tell people what has happened.
The people cry,
Their sorrow unmeasured.

Let not those trucks roll on unchallenged,
Smoke flying up after them,
It must be stopped.
A silent quarry, the peace disturbed.

Laurent Stephenson (13)
Royal Latin School, Buckingham

Never To Wake

Dragged, silently, lonely and desperately,
Down to the water the disappeared are taken.
During the night in the dark, dank and smelly,
Into the water . . . never to waken!

Down to the water the disappeared and taken,
Women and children and men by the score.
Into the water . . . never to waken,
The guards leave the scene to the prisons, for more.

Women and children and men by the score,
Crying, dying, they stand by the lake.
The guards leave the scene to the prisons, for more.
The prisoners, dead . . . they never will wake!

Crying, dying, they stand by the lake.
During the night in the dark, dank and smelly,
The prisoners, dead . . . they never will wake!
Dragged, silently, lonely and desperately.

Charlie Calver (13)
Royal Latin School, Buckingham

Nature Stroll

We knew what was beyond
The berry-trodden lane but had we really looked?
As we cast our fresh eyes over nature around us,
We noticed much more than before.
Had the leaves always stretched across like a canopy?
Had the birds always sang in that array of notes?
Had the ripples in the lake always made such a gentle pattern?
Had those lilac flowers always been there to contrast with the
                                          emerald leaves?
Had the trees been this lush every June?
Had the lake always reflected the bank as clear as a mirror?
We knew the answer was yes,
But we had never really looked before.

Katie Reynolds (16)
St Mark's West Essex Catholic School, Harlow

SATs

I sat there,
I stared,
I looked around
And continued to glare,
My head's somewhere else,
This is the most anxious
I have ever felt.
I look at my friends
They're self-assured.
Oh no, I don't know this stupid word.
It's so quiet,
I can't stand it
And I'm failing
To remember this stupid stuff.
I begin to sweat and hum in my head.
Then it all comes flooding back.

Kelly Whalley (14)
St Mark's West Essex Catholic School, Harlow

The Neglected Graveyard

For nine centuries the church has stood tall,
Looming over the dead like a loyal guard,
But now, left crumbling it lies in decay,
The only ancient sight left in a modern town.

The rumble of traffic sounds in the distance,
Yet the graveyard remains completely motionless.
The rain has weathered the lines of headstones,
Fading the names of those long forgotten.

Moss climbs up the brickwork like an acrobat,
As fingers of mist envelop the landscape.
Weeds and nettles grow out of control,
The graveyard remains derelict and in decay.

Emma Bell (15)
St Mark's West Essex Catholic School, Harlow

Netteswell Pond

The summer sun beats down on the muggy June morning,
The light glistens on the rippling water,
The ducks along the back all line up like Olympic swimmers
Ready to start a race.
Crowd cheers are the birds chirping whilst the spectators
Are the rising reeds.
As you walk around the pond you see one lone heron in the middle,
As if it were king.
The overgrown plants close in on the arch
Which leads to the abandoned graveyard,
Broken stones, dying flowers,
'John Carder, died 1882' reads one mouldy stone.
Walking around the lonely, sad graveyard
The abandoned church gives off a spooky atmosphere,
Could the souls of the people lying in the yard be hiding there,
Watching the living pass by?
Back out by the pond, fishermen relax nearby
Sunken into the bank's plants, ready to catch the next big fish
And all the nature and beauty of the pond
Spoiled by litter,
Spoiled by graffiti,
Spoiled by man.

Kayleigh Henderson (15)
St Mark's West Essex Catholic School, Harlow

The Tiger

I live beneath the long grass of Asia,
I prowl along searching for meat.
My bright fur will dazzle in your eye,
Black and white or orange.
I smell my prey in the sweltering sun,
And see the flesh rip in my mind.
The other animals hear my call,
And run for shelter near or far
For they are all scared of the *tiger!*

Sian Gentry (13)
St Mark's West Essex Catholic School, Harlow

Paradise Pond

The tunnel of overhanging trees shaped like the pond's archway,
Light seeped through the ceiling, speckling the rugged trail.

Pollen wafted aimlessly in the humid air,
Drifting without purpose in the silence and calmness.

The willow dropped low, like a curtain,
Hiding the pathway to a beautiful paradise.

Trees framed this nirvana, like a scenic picture,
Protecting this heaven with their far-reaching limbs.

The pond reflected the sun like a sheet of glass,
Constructing a dance floor for the waltzing dragonflies.

Ranks of ducks lined in single file, preparing to march,
Upholders of peace in the tranquil waters.

Fishes leap out of the water in exhibition,
Sending wavering ripples to the edge of the pool.

The angler stared intently at the still water,
Waiting patiently for the precise moment to strike.

Leaving, I heard the echoes of the stagnant pond.
Nature's orchestra performed its farewell symphony.

Fu-Wah Kwong (15)
St Mark's West Essex Catholic School, Harlow

Nature - Haikus

Yellow, green flower,
Colourful as the sunshine,
A beautiful smell.

A smooth and green stem
Green blossom, that makes you sneeze
Oval fresh petals.

Autumn tree, gold leaves,
Many leaves fall from the trees,
Warm and comforting.

Gregory Ashoori (14)
St Mark's West Essex Catholic School, Harlow

Work Experience

Work experience,
Scared, looking forward to it,
And can't wait to start.

At school, Purford Green,
The atmosphere was friendly,
My first day was great.

Halfway through the week,
I've met a lot of children,
And learnt a lot too.

My last day at school,
Taught maths and literacy,
With the class teacher.

Now it has ended
I can reflect on it all,
Work experience was an experience worthwhile.

Toni Cleary (15)
St Mark's West Essex Catholic School, Harlow

Work Experience

A different routine from every day,
No chance for break, chance to play.

Messing about put on hold,
Two weeks, breaking the mould.

At a desk, in a garage or playroom,
Office work, fixing cars or making balloons.

A new experience, chance to learn,
Time out from school, a different turn.

A new meaning to working life,
Understanding the chances took, roll of the dice.

Holly Bailey (15)
St Mark's West Essex Catholic School, Harlow

Summer Morning

Summer berries crush underfoot as I stroll along the tree-shaded path,
Birds sing their summer morning song,
A gentle breeze lightly brushes my face,
I head towards the still, peaceful pond.

The water glistens in the summer sun,
Ducks line up along the pond's edge as if they are unsure of the water.
The heron stands, alone, eyeing the fish beneath him;
The pretty, pink flowers contrast against dark green leaves;
Creeping ivy slowly climbs up the old, red brick wall.

As I enter the graveyard my feelings start to change:
The graves look abandoned,
The pathway cracked and winding,
The old church is locked up.
My happy mood disappears and I am glum.

Claudette James (15)
St Mark's West Essex Catholic School, Harlow

My Poem

The predatory cheetah, sleek and silent,
Hunting for its prey, in the darkness,
Creeps up on its foe, getting silent and more silent, less and less . . .
Its dark red eyes, flash in the moonlight,
Moving up toward the bird, before it takes flight.
He tenses his claws and hunches his back,
The bird's senses are turning slack,
It relaxes and sings, thinking all kinds of things,
And then suddenly stops, it can feel the cheetah's breath,
On the back of its neck, it takes flight,
But the claws swipe,
It cannot breathe, it just wants to leave,
But feels its fangs sinking into his neck,
Then . . . darkness.

Hayden Lester (13)
St Mark's West Essex Catholic School, Harlow

Rest In Peace

I wonder what this path will be like
In a hundred years,
With the view so bright and so brilliant;
The sound - so clear - of newborn birds
Crying out for their parents to come home.

Will the reflection of the appearing pond
Have the same vivid image,
With fishermen at its edge striking and missing at their leisure?
The woman with her young
Child passing along the path, stopping,
Looking at the quick bird
Gliding across
The pond *destroying* the *brilliance* of the scene,
Then finally entering the lost graveyard . . .

I wonder what this place will be like
In a hundred years?
Will the grass be so long that the woman
And her child
Cannot pass?

Will the gravestones sink deeper and deeper and deeper
Into the sacred ground?
Will the crumbling walls completely fall
Blocking the *entrances* and the *exits*?
Will it matter if the forgotten ground is never recognisable again
Or will only the obliviously innocent, white butterfly
Land on the moss-covered graves of the long deceased?

Dominic Steingold (15)
St Mark's West Essex Catholic School, Harlow

The Churchyard

The churchyard seems so empty;
The sinking gravestones,
The crumbling wall,
The overgrown garden locked away from prying eyes by a rusting gate,
Seem to hark back to a time when people cared.

Now, only the occasional visitor;
Walking the dog,
Taking a stroll,
Trudging through on the way to meet friends,
Passes through their mind elsewhere, or perhaps reflecting
On how pleasant the scene is.

And it is pleasant;
The wall, though crumbling, is picturesque,
The garden, though overgrown, is overflowing with intriguing charm,
And the silence affords a peaceful quality.

So why?
Why is litter strewn carelessly, plucked,
From one grave to another by the gentle breeze?
Why is the wall adorned, not just by cracked mortar and
                                          bedraggled moss,
But scrawled with graffiti too?

The churchyard seems so empty;
The sinking gravestones,
The crumbling wall,
The overgrown garden locked away from prying eyes by a rusting gate,
Seem to hark back to a time when people cared.

Matt Stent (15)
St Mark's West Essex Catholic School, Harlow

The Horse

The horse walks out from the trees,
Leaving behind his friends eating grass.
He walks majestically to the gate,
Where his owner awaits to catch him.

She slips the head collar over his nose,
And does the buckle up by his ear.
She walks him down to the hose,
Where she washes his dusty feet.

She then brushes his body clean,
Until his coat gleams and shines.
Then she slips his saddle on keen,
Does up the girth and gets ready to ride.

She walks him loosely on each rein,
Then trots him rhythmically round the school.
Then she canters on a circle,
And then jumps a jump to finish.

Walking around to cool him down,
She then untacks him in his box.
She rubs him down and gives him a treat
Of Polos, carrots and an apple or two.

Ross Crisp (13)
St Mark's West Essex Catholic School, Harlow

Chrysanthemum - Haikus

The chrysanthemum
Shines sunshine through me, fresh buds
Grow to full beauty.

Autumn tree sheds brown,
Crusty, crumbling, crackling leaves
That I step onto.

Winter tree covered
In snow, the roofs are buried
Under white blanket.

Thomas Verbrugge (14)
St Mark's West Essex Catholic School, Harlow

A Distant Dream

Strolling around, tall and proud, the Siberian tiger roams,
The soft stripy fur, against the white snow, it's the territory he owns.
With pale grey eyes and black and white stripes, added to beautiful
pearly teeth.
An amazing creature, so precious and rare, disappearing one by one.
Great big men, who come around, barging about the world,
With guns and swords,
He runs, he roars,
His feet pound silently on the snow,
But the poachers, they'll find him,
The poachers, they know.
They're on his trail now,
And he's in their sight,
With a shot of the gun and a searing pain,
The tiger slows his pace
With his world going black.
The Siberian tiger lays down,
The poachers, they've killed him,
The poachers, they've won . . .

Catherine Moranda (13)
St Mark's West Essex Catholic School, Harlow

SATs

The SATs are over,
It's time to throw the books away.
No more revision. No more learning.
So say goodbye to multiplications,
Smash your test tubes and eat your tasty adjectives
Because the SATs are over.
So put your feet up and relax.
All these dreams,
All these plans,
I did them all with these two hands.
The SATs are brainteasers
And they won't please you!

Abe Pardue (14)
St Mark's West Essex Catholic School, Harlow

Poem

We have to sit our SATs test,
They're coming up next week,
We have to do our best now
To get the groups we seek.

We have to keep revising,
The date is getting near.
The nails are getting shorter,
Getting bitten with the fear.

The tests are now tomorrow,
I'm getting really worried.
We won't be in the class all day
But at least we won't be hurried.

I've got all my equipment.
Here goes, I've got my pen,
No more late revision,
Let's sort the boys from men.

And now the tests are over,
No pressure anymore.
There's nothing but relief
And I'm first out the door.

Tom Scanlon (13)
St Mark's West Essex Catholic School, Harlow

Monkey

M ischievous and mysterious
O n the rampage all the time
N ever takes a rest from playing
K nows people are coming to look
E very day it swings and jumps and plays
Y es! It's the best animal in the world.

Lee Webster (13)
St Mark's West Essex Catholic School, Harlow

It's A Jungle Out There

Giraffes are skinny and tall,
Elephants are so very huge,
Piglets are so fat and small,
Monkeys act just like a stooge.

Walking through the zoo
With nothing I can do,
Seeing animals in a cage
Being locked up for an age.

Animals in there till they die,
Chickens made into chicken pie,
But it's not all up to me,
They are there for all to see.

I think keeping animals is cruel,
I don't support zoos at all.
They should be released where weather is mild,
All released into the wild.

Niall O'Sullivan (13)
St Mark's West Essex Catholic School, Harlow

What Am I?

I'm black and scary
But very hairy.

When I get a stitch
I start to itch.

I like to eat
my tasty treat.

Beating my chest
Means I'm the best.
What am I?

A gorilla.

Zahra Ali (13)
St Mark's West Essex Catholic School, Harlow

The SATs

I'm sweaty and nervous, sticky and tense,
My mind's gone blank, surely I'm not that dense.
No wait it's back, thank the Lord for that,
I looked at books, and sat and sat . . .

My eyes as bloodshot as red as could be,
It'll be over soon, I can get back to normality.
The time has come, I think my brain will burst
With all the knowledge, still some will go with the first.

Midweek now, it seems never-ending,
I've curvature of the spine with all of that bending.
My hand aches with all the shakes,
As for the brain, it shouts, *'Give me a break!'*

I've done, it's finished, it's over for good
And have I done the best I could?
I tried as hard as I could and more,
Whatever the result I know that for sure.

James Smith (13)
St Mark's West Essex Catholic School, Harlow

Homework

At my first day of school,
I thought it would be cool,
It was bigger than the last,
My brother told me it would go fast.
Slowly we move class to class,
Me and my mates are all having a laugh,
Me and my friends sit on one table,
Listening to a teacher's Greek fable.
Lunchtime is the best part of the day,
We all play football that day in May.
As the school finishes fast,
Me and my mates say *school was a blast!*

Daniel Goddard (12)
St Mark's West Essex Catholic School, Harlow

The Wolf

The wolf, the wild dog
Appears through the fog,
Jumping over fallen logs.

He is hungry, you can see,
It is clear to you and me.

Stalking prey, ready to kill,
Making sure, it is not ill,
Hours later, stalking still.

Very soon he will eat.
He will get a bit of meat,
Never, ever, taking a seat.

Seeing the wolf, the prey,
It is running away
But the wolf, it has no time to stay.

The prey is in the bag
And the wolf shall never feel sad.

The wolf, the wild dog.

Stewart Potter (13)
St Mark's West Essex Catholic School, Harlow

SATs Poem

SATs is a word
I wish I'd never heard,
It comes around each year
And fills us with dread and fear.
Tests, exams and questions to answer,
Will I get good marks?
I hope, but may need a transfer
To a nice, warm place where I can relax.
SATs will be over, a thing of the past,
No revising, no more SATs at last.

Danielle Murphy (13)
St Mark's West Essex Catholic School, Harlow

Komodo Dragon

Komodo dragons
Are brave and strong.
Komodo dragons
Are never wrong.

Komodo dragons
Are fierce and fast.
Komodo dragons
Never come last.

Komodo dragons
Are sturdy and tough.
Komodo dragons
Are green and rough.

Komodo dragons
Are not kind *or* caring
And claws are the only
Thing they like sharing.

Elizabeth Shaw (13)
St Mark's West Essex Catholic School, Harlow

SATs

This silent absence calls to me
As minutes tick by mockingly,
The very quiet cuts me deep
And every statement makes me weep,
Dark pressure poisons every nerve -
To what use will all this serve?
My fingers shake as I complete
The questions that I can't delete,
As rustling papers, clicking pens,
Scraping pencils and blots I cleanse,
Remind me that I've lost all hope,
I ask why they thought I could cope.

Sumana Begum (13)
St Mark's West Essex Catholic School, Harlow

SATs

Waiting, listening for my name to be called.
Am I next?
Different names echoing
In my ears, Cory, Cox, Davis.

Blood running cold,
Mind goes blank,
Hands start to shake,
I can't do this.

Rising from my seat,
All eyes on me.
Opening the doors,
Blinded by the light,
Not a sound, silence.

I sit down, what next?

Sun rays shining
Through the bars on the windows,
Guards at every exit,
How can I escape?

Footsteps echo
Through the hall,
I close my eyes and imagine
Running out the door.

SATs, SATs, SATs,
Meaning one thing,
Scary Abnormal Tests!

Danielle De Cruz (13)
St Mark's West Essex Catholic School, Harlow

Butter - Haiku

Butter is slippy
It slip, slides around the plate
You spread it on toast.

Thomas Day (13)
St Mark's West Essex Catholic School, Harlow

SATs

English
It's not so bad
Writing up Shakespeare
Driving teachers mad.

Maths
Make time for revision
Going over basics
Plus, times and division.

Science
Is the worst of all three
I would get a tutor
But can't afford the fee.

A mix of emotions
Comes flooding to me
Thinking of these tests
How important they can be.

Putting nerves aside
While going to the test
All I need is to stay positive
I'll be the best!

Katie Oliver (13)
St Mark's West Essex Catholic School, Harlow

My Dogs

My dogs are so cute and lovely,
They are so cuddly.
One is small and hairy,
The other one's tall and not scary.
I want to stay with them forever,
They will never leave ever!
I can't wait to get home,
I don't want them to be left on their own.

Sarah Nulty (12)
St Mark's West Essex Catholic School, Harlow

SATs

As May begins to dawn,
Fun comes to an end,
The season that makes all children mourn,
The SATs are round the bend!

Three lessons are to be learned,
Each one a tale of woe,
Some are left scarred and burnt,
Their fate like Banquo!

Study Shakespeare's play
And learn how Macbeth died,
Take in maths formulae,
The end is almost nigh!

Now for something so complex,
The science of our lives,
Now there is nothing next to learn,
You can hear the distant cries!

There it sits all neatly packed,
The horror that awaits,
The SATs so proudly stacked,
As I step through Hell's gates!

Thomas Mintoff (13)
St Mark's West Essex Catholic School, Harlow

SATs

SATs are good,
SATs are fun
But they're not always fun for everyone.

SATs are alright,
SATs are OK,
You just have to think they're only here for a day!

SATs are a pain,
SATs are annoying,
There's nothing new, they're just so boring.

Georgia Gadsdon (14)
St Mark's West Essex Catholic School, Harlow

My School Is Changing

Now look here, my school is changing,
The colours are rearranging.

Look at our new Miss,
Scary! She seems to hiss.

The subjects adding and dividing,
Would I be better off just hiding?

'Stop that!'
'Quick here comes Sir!'
Will he have a go at her?

The boy sits at his table sleeping,
The teacher's so mad he's nearly weeping.

The bricks in which we are enclosed,
No joy, no land to be exposed.

The dark corridor scares us all,
This school isn't all that small.

Look at Sir cough,
I guess he isn't all that tough.

Our days are filled with many subjects,
Look at all those lonely rejects.

I can safely say that my school is changing,
Even my pen I am exchanging.

I don't want to preach revolution,
My school has undergone evolution.

Theo Ancient (12)
St Mark's West Essex Catholic School, Harlow

Victory Calls

As fast as it can go
The wild roar goes,
Keen eyes upon the green
Never taking off sight . . .
Yellow skin over him,
Black dots hide him,
Step by step,
Blink and gone,
Run far, run fast,
Victory calls,
No one as fast,
Finally, won!
Mouth full and tired,
Turning home,
Over the orange sky
To a dark road,
Move on, go far.
Home is near.
Dark and hungry,
Little yaps
Call from the far,
So they don't starve
He gives his victory yaps.
Dark sky,
Time of cold,
Warm up, heat up,
Dream well, dream deep,
Tomorrow a new sun,
Tomorrow a new run.

Vanessa Heilbron (15)
St Mark's West Essex Catholic School, Harlow

Jungle

Deep in the jungle in the middle of the night
There are animals wanting a fight.
You can't disturb them
Or they will get annoyed with you.

Then out of the pitch-black sky
Came a swarm of bees flying high.
You run for cover just to hide
And then you hear the sound of the seaside tide.

You're just imagining it and the bees are gone,
But there is something new and it's four yards long,
It's green and black and on the floor,
Oh no, it's a snake and poisonous too.

It slithered through the grass towards me,
The snake stopped to eat its prey, I was so scared I dropped my key,
I picked it up and ran away, then to see a tiger
It stood up in front of me.

I looked around and saw my house
But the tiger made me feel like a mouse.
It looked at me and then moved away,
That was enough for another day.

Christopher Munden (12)
St Mark's West Essex Catholic School, Harlow

The SATs

SATs are boring,
They become so annoying.

Always there every day of the week.
I wish they could vanish with a squeak.

They are always there when you don't want them.
Always starting about ten.
We don't like the SATs,
They're so annoying, just like rats!

James Rose (14)
St Mark's West Essex Catholic School, Harlow

Starting Saint Mark's

I didn't know what to expect,
As I walked through those gates.
Would I settle in?
Would I make some mates?

Mr Brunwin said his piece
Welcoming us all,
Thousands of new faces
Crammed into one hall.

Me and my mates
Now have another change,
Getting ready for Year 8
Higher up in the school.

Overall I like Saint Mark's,
All my friends
They never keep me in the dark,
It's non-stop fun.

Rebecca Burnage (12)
St Mark's West Essex Catholic School, Harlow

School

S aying goodbye to my bestest friend,
C losing my school books for the very last time,
H oly Cross days are at an end.
O h how I hope we keep in touch,
O ther ways to get to school,
L ost, I hope not.

S tarting school is easy,
T ime goes by quite quick.

M y new friend's as good as old,
A ll my homework done when set,
R eading on Tuesdays, better not forget.
K eeping my contact book tidy,
S ettled in, that's me now.

Sarah Crehan (12)
St Mark's West Essex Catholic School, Harlow

Thou Art A Poem About A School

Thou art a poem about a school,
Where children learned through plays of duels,
But the plays that delighted them the best,
Were Shakespeare's plays of conquest,
'Hamlet' and his treacherous deeds,
Of the 'Taming of the Shrew'.
Shakespeare's comedies they laughed at too.

In their minds the scene was set,
The clashing swords, the fatal step,
Through bad and good they fought on strong,
Waiting for the witches' song,
Of bleeding hearts through battles won,
Of kings and queens and lonesome sons.

And in the Globe Shakespeare's visions appeared,
Of doomed love and wept tears,
And now at the setting of the sun,
This woeful poem was begun.

Natalie Bell (12)
St Mark's West Essex Catholic School, Harlow

First Day Of School

The look of horror on her face again,
Whenever school is mentioned again.
The kicking, screaming mornings again
That lead up to school again,
The hours of dressing again
And then it is school again.
The drive to school again,
The cheering when school comes again,
The booing at weekends again,
The dressing in the mornings again,
Then yahoo,
It's school again.

Esther Kingsmill (12)
St Mark's West Essex Catholic School, Harlow

Crocodile

His scaly skin stands out
In the swamp.
His eyes a cold dark green.

Crouching so lowly,
Deep in the swamp
He is all alone.

Animals fear him,
He has no friends.
All the other crocodiles
Drive him round the bend.

He's different than them
And does not like to kill.
The rest of the crocodiles
Think it's a skill.

The crocodiles think
He's stupid,
He doesn't want to
Be their friend at all.

Sarah Comerford (12)
St Mark's West Essex Catholic School, Harlow

School Day Tomorrow

School bag, check, uniform, check,
It's a school day tomorrow, got to be ready.
Pencil case, check, school shoes, check,
It's a school day tomorrow, got to be ready.
Correct equipment, check, otherwise the teacher will moan!
This time tomorrow I will be home,
Wait a minute, I will be home! It's *Saturday* tomorrow!

Karen O'Callaghan (11)
St Mark's West Essex Catholic School, Harlow

School

Boring maths,
Difficult sum,
Hot, stuffy classroom,
Everyone's glum.

Sitting, daydreaming,
Thinking of tea.
It won't be long,
Till half-past three.

It happens at last,
The bell rings.
'It's home time,'
Everyone sings.

Pushing, shoving,
Sliding across the floor,
Everyone's desperate
To reach the door.

Crowds of children
Swarm the street.
The road is busy,
Some mums they meet.

Thinning away, thinning away,
Stragglers there are plenty.
Thinning away till all are gone,
The road is quiet and empty.

Elise Turnell (12)
St Mark's West Essex Catholic School, Harlow

SATs Poem

We are all waiting outside
Looking at the hall,
With a mix of emotions,
Of fear, nervous and dull.

We are called in alphabetically,
As, then Bs, then Cs,
And before I know it,
F is called, 'that's me'.

I sit down at a table,
In the centre of the hall,
Waiting for what's to come,
As nervous as all.

We are handed our papers
And on people's faces I saw death,
Oh no,
It's Macbeth.

Half an hour gone already
And I haven't written a lot,
Everybody has written
Much more than I have got.

I glance up at the clock,
Ten minutes to go,
What do I know about Macbeth?
Oh, I don't know.

Five minutes to go,
I have to read over my test,
The first line doesn't make sense,
What about the rest?

That's it, test over,
I have failed in my eyes.
You know what I think?
I should have revised!

Callum Fitzpatrick (12)
St Mark's West Essex Catholic School, Harlow

I Didn't Know What To Think

I was scared,
I was nervous,
I didn't know what to think.

I was happy,
I was excited,
I didn't know what to think.

I made new friends,
I met new people,
But still didn't know what to think.

I settled down,
I got on with my work,
But even now
I don't know what to think.

Jade Clarke (11)
St Mark's West Essex Catholic School, Harlow

School

My school is a pathway to Hell,
From the beginning of class to the end-of-day bell.
For starters there are lions at the gate,
They have big, sharp teeth and bite you if you're late!

The teachers are like monsters, fierce and scary,
They have warts on their noses, which are very, very hairy!

The punishment are by far the worst,
Just the mention of them makes your insides burst.
Like fetching and carrying heavy loads,
And eating the eyes and legs of toads!

So, to be honest, if I were you,
I'd stay away from the school and the teachers too!

Louise Chapman (12)
St Mark's West Essex Catholic School, Harlow

Starting A New School

B eing woken up really early - *groan!*
E agerly wanting it to be home time.
G etting ready for school,
I n the car ready to go.
N ot sure about the uniform.
N ot knowing where to go when we get there
I n the hall where all the Year 7 were.
N ewman is my form, which is the best.
G oing to our first class was quite scary and exciting.

O ff to our second lesson it seems to go on forever!
F inished our lessons, now off to break - *yum!*

S een other children scared like you and me.
E agerly wanting it to be home time.
C oming to our next lesson wondering what it could be.
O pening our exercise books,
N oticing the new rooms,
D oing harder work but we can cope,
A rriving to the class on time,
R egistration time every morning and after lunch,
Y ear 7 is one big step.

S itting down in our chair learning.
C hurch in the school is really great, saying prayers to the Lord.
H oping we learn something new.
O pening our contact books to write our homework
O nly five lessons a day - *ya!*
L ast day until the summer term is very far away.

Kate Allaway (12)
St Mark's West Essex Catholic School, Harlow

New At School

All these classes
That are new to you,
People have gone through them
And so will you.
Books to keep,
Homework to be done,
But don't worry
It can be fun.
Names of teachers,
Friends you don't know,
You should try and learn them,
So give it a go.
The school can be big,
But nothing to fear
There's always a friend,
Or a teacher that's near.
Now it's time for school,
Good luck on your way,
Just have a happy face
And a smile every day.

Robyn Fryer (11)
St Mark's West Essex Catholic School, Harlow

Silent Tears

My words fell on silent ears,
Just like they always do,
My words fell quiet, ignored,
Like drops of rain from sky,
My words fell on hardened hearts,
Met with no compassion.

My words fell on silent ears,
Of course they always do,
My words fell like silent thunder,
But to me my words were everything,
My words fell with silent tears.

My tears,
My tears alone,
Why don't they care?
Why don't they cry?
Their silence shuns my silent tears,
But still, they fall with my now silent words.

Emma Garrett (15)
Soham Village College, Soham

Genre For Our Generation

'You do not have to say anything, but it may harm your
Defence if you fail to . . .'
Stop. Repeat. Slam.
Stupid pigs always on my tail.
Story of truth. Caused by lies.

You think they're your mates . . .
Stab you, hate you. In disguise.
Run.
Hole in your pocket.
Shot.
One in your head.
Drop . . . dead.

Step into a cage,
The life of another man.
Regret.
Not forgiven . . . And never
Forget.

Not guilty.
Run from authority, run away from yourself,
But there's no turning back.
Your hand will hide your pride, but it won't hide the shame.

Rebecca Hamilton (15)
Southend High School for Girls, Westcliff-on-Sea

Mrs Lightyear

To infinity and beyond. Indeed.
Being a space ranger's wife isn't all it's cracked up to be.
Star Command calls, 'He's off.'
Typical. Saving the world one toy at a time from the 'Evil Emperor Zurg'
Staying at home, changing batteries for the neighbours.
If I have to rewrite his catchphrase buttons one more time
And then sit there and listen to 'Buzz Lightyear to the rescue'
Over and over again.
I'll give him catchphrases. I do find it strange that I can't catch him
When it's time to go food shopping.
If he spent half the time with me as he does with the Universe
Protection Unit, life would be a lot nicer.
When will I see infinity or beyond?
Trapped within these four walls. All alone.
When will I soar through the skies, arm stretched out,
Wings fully extended?
Watching Woody lose his hat is the highlight of my day.
And him?
He's off at space camp. With Andy. Campfires. Smores.
Smore like the noticeable space in the bed.
Where does that leave me?
At home, cleaning the rocket.

Sophie Bruce (15)
Southend High School for Girls, Westcliff-on-Sea

Message In A Bottle

Click.

He came in and slammed the door,
Threw his coat upon the peg. Stop.
Told me to make dinner. Perhaps he's
Had a hard day at work. Yes. That's happened before.

Dinner isn't quick enough.
Today I can't cook. Every day is today.
He barks about the house. I didn't do enough cleaning. Perhaps
He's had a hard day at work. Yes, maybe.

His hip flask, near empty - held in its leash,
Moves to the study. I hardly notice.
Obediently, I wipe up the kitchen floor.
It wasn't always like this. Before.

Before his job got really stressful and
I became so lazy.
Before my face became colourful
And our relationship so hazy.

He was a wonderful man, any excuse to celebrate,
Christmas, birthdays then eventually just because we had a great life.
'There's nothing wrong with enjoying yourself,' he'd say in
                                                         good humour.
Everything was in good humour. Before.

I went into the hall and fetched his coat.
A weight pulled it down - maybe his conscience.
And there it was. I took it out and placed it
On the table.

There it stood. Sunlight filtered into the room,
The small bottle of whisky stood on the table.
It triggered.
The message was loud and clear.

Click.

Sophia Bathgate (15)
Southend High School for Girls, Westcliff-on-Sea

A Night Like No Other

A mansion in the dark,
Empty, deserted, cold,
Not scared at all,
It was only a lark.

I head up the drive,
Gravel crunching underneath,
The building up ahead
Looking as if alive.

A squeaky door
Or was it a scream?
How could I tell?
I couldn't be sure.

An empty room,
Portraits on the walls
All screaming with fear
As if they are seeing doom.

Footsteps behind me,
I'm frozen with fear,
Wanting to run,
To break free.

I wake up on a floor,
It was all a dream,
But the portraits are still there,
Pointing at the door.

I don't turn around
There's only one exit,
It was blocked -
By death.

Paul Watson (14)
The Colne Community School, Brightlingsea

The Future

I looked into the future
As far as I could see,
Through summer's lull and winter's chill
To see what I could be.

A doctor or an artist,
A salesman or a preacher?
An actor or a botanist
Or possibly a teacher?

I looked into the future
And saw my family.
My loving wife and children
And my eternity.

Henry Beresford (12)
The Perse School, Cambridge

The Future

Garbage pipes and clogged up drains,
Acid falls whenever it rains.
Earthquakes and thunderstorms,
None care but the Earth still mourns.

Mud and slime fills every street,
The despair is clear in all you meet.
Smoke and dust fills the air,
All nature dies but Bush doesn't care.

We must prevent this inevitable doom,
We must prevent this before the Earth goes *boom!*

William Parker (12)
The Perse School, Cambridge

Nuclear

The greatest act of destruction
The world had ever seen;
The human race extinguished
But that had been foreseen.

Nature isn't something
That should be tampered with.
You cannot use it for your ways
And still be allowed to live.

Look where science got them,
Look what they had done.
They created a weapon
With the power of the sun.

Yes, a great invention,
But a tool for waging war;
Everybody used them
And now the Earth's no more.

For that is what has happened
And we are still in shock,
A nuclear war has been and gone
And the Earth's a lifeless rock.

Max Hewitt (11)
The Perse School, Cambridge

Is This The Future?

Floating cars,
Men on Mars,
Is this the future?

Aliens in society
In all their variety,
Is this the future?

Shining robots,
Other whatnots,
Is this the future?

No more forests,
But plastic florists,
Is this the future?

We're running out of oil,
We're causing total turmoil,
Is this the future?

William Raynaud (11)
The Perse School, Cambridge

The Future

In the future there are futurised cars
And floating bars.
There are futurised trains
And supersonic planes.

The people are robots with funny hair
And to see a bird is really quite rare.
There is loads of pollution in the air
And we wiped out birds, which is not fair.

The humans destroyed our lovely Earth,
We have ruined where we lived, our only turf.
So let's start again, without a fight
And now what is wrong, we will turn right.

Daniel Vasa (13)
The Sweyne Park School, Rayleigh

A Tree's Lament

I've seen many changes in my life,
First I was dropped by a jay in a lush, green field,
The other trees were all happy,
But now the country around me has been killed.

I sprung strong roots
That grew stronger and stronger,
Then my body pushed out of the ground
And grew longer and longer.

Sun and rain have given me life,
The squirrels and birds, my friends,
My branches a haven for all living things,
It seemed my happiness would never end.

After five hundred years I could finally see the world in all its glory,
I saw the seasons come and go,
My acorns would grow and drop to the ground,
And under my branches I saw the children grow.

And now I'm old and choked by fumes,
My leaves are burnt by acid rain,
I no longer live in a lush, green field,
And constantly feel the pain.

Now I'm surrounded by factories and motorways,
And watching the other trees die,
Now I'm sad, no longer happy,
And sigh a long miserable sigh.

Does mankind realise what he is doing to the Earth?
The land will be dull and dry,
Soon there will be nothing at all,
And all I can do is feel helpless and watch the world die.

Bethany Elmer (11)
The Sweyne Park School, Rayleigh

Holiday Diary

A holiday to Tenerife, a family of four,
I was jumping with joy as I stepped out the door.
It didn't matter to me that I had been there before,
A holiday twice, I couldn't ask for anything more.

Scuba-diving in the deep blue sea,
All the emotions, as happy as can be.
The water's clean and blue like the sky,
The excitement I was feeling as the fishes swam by.

Miniature golf and seaside games,
The dads have to win; it's always the same.
After the games, it's dinner by the beach,
A three-course meal and a cocktail each.

A walk to the shops, there's gifts to get,
Then we head to the hotel to watch the sunset.
We're down at the bar, beside the pool,
Mum's had a brandy and now acting a fool.

A jousting knight and a pirates evening,
The purple knight, mmm, my heart he was stealing.
A show with The Drifters is always good fun,
It seemed strange that we all knew the songs they had sung.

My sister's off to the pool again,
The boys were calling, she's not to blame.
I want to play tennis, so I need her now,
She's not to be found, I've lost her somehow.

The holiday's over and it's time to pack,
But I know somehow, one day I'll be back.
We finally get home, straight off to bed,
I fall asleep with Tenerife in my head.

Michaela Galea (13)
The Sweyne Park School, Rayleigh

The Future?

In the future we will not have the things we have now,
We will have smaller, advanced gadgets, even machines that mop
your brow.

The latest stuff now will be the old-fashioned things then,
People will use robots instead of a pencil or pen.

People will live longer and lead better lives,
But people will have robots instead of their wives.

We will live underwater and adapt to our scene,
Robots will do everything like cooking and be able to clean.

Mobile phones will be the size of big ants,
Hopefully the robots will clean up our pants.

All these things could come true,
We could have robots and an electric loo.

Maybe I am really pushing to the extreme,
But I am having fun in this futuristic dream!

Laura Thornton (12)
The Sweyne Park School, Rayleigh

The Future

What's the year 2020 going to be like?

A re you going to be the owner of an untidy house,

R odents all over the place and a giant woodlouse.
O verrun by too many mice.
B eing this kind of owner will not be very nice!
O nly one thing will stop this . . .
T hey'll be the only solution.

B ut what will these things be?
U gly and grumpy will they be?
T hey may be sweet and kind,
L ovely with a good mind.
E xcept, what will they be . . .
R obot butlers?

Rachel Steddon (11)
The Sweyne Park School, Rayleigh

The Future

I wonder what the future will show,
You can keep on thinking but you'll never know.

It might be hot, it might be cold,
Babies might even be born old.

There might even be flying cars around,
But until then they will stay on the ground.

You may even get a couple of clones
And they will be all flesh and bones.

You might even see flying prams,
And also don't forget holograms.

Now poverty has disappeared,
And now women can also have beards.

I wonder what the future will show,
Will Michael Jackson ever sort out his nose?

Will we ever run out of petrol?
Will there ever be a flying kettle?

Will everything be run by solar power
And will there ever be any more flowers?

I wonder what the future will show?
You can keep on thinking but you will never know.

Chris Callahan (12)
The Sweyne Park School, Rayleigh

Out The Window

I looked out the window at the dark, gloomy clouds,
And the lightning thundering down like hammer and nails.
The raindrops as they fell from the sky,
As the dark, gloomy clouds turned about to die.
Then all of a sudden the sky turned grey,
By the ghosts of midnight some people say.
Out of the window I saw a white gleam,
Coming closer and closer
I didn't know what I had seen.
A ghost, a ghoul or a vampire,
This thing started shouting, 'You liar, you liar.'
I started shaking, I screamed out loud,
I have done what you desired, how have I failed?
It was standing right next to me,
It grabbed my arms, my legs, my knees.
Then I was stuck, him holding me tight,
I struggled and struggled with all my might.
Then all of a sudden, my eyes opened up,
Was I in Heaven or Hell, or was I just stuck?
Next to me was my mum, she wasn't dead,
I was alive, sleeping in my bed.
It must have been a nightmare,
That really gave me a scare.

Emma Tarling (12)
The Sweyne Park School, Rayleigh

The End Of The World

It is the year five million, the world has come to an end,
The sun is about to swallow Earth - this is it my friend.
Death, we're all going to die,
Incineration, burning while we lie,
A wall of fire is coming,
Screams in my head, they are drumming,
An explosion of heat has struck,
This is it - here I'm stuck,
Further and further it lurches,
No one to help or propose searches.
Here it is, the sun,
It is all done.
I am gone.

Rachel Hudson (12)
The Sweyne Park School, Rayleigh

The Future

The future is the unknown,
Things left to our imagination.
Are there aliens? Is there a reason
To life, learning, school and work?
Will those we love be gone one day
Or do we just refuse to believe it?

All I know is that life will go on,
When I die, when we all die.
Life will go on forever.

Lucinda Hughes (12)
The Sweyne Park School, Rayleigh

Future Thoughts

What lies ahead in the future,
For us, the globe and nature?
Global warming is one example,
Can this be fixed?

Some days we look forward to,
Like holidays, the weekend and sometimes school.
Great discoveries and new inventions,
Help us live and maybe make the world a better place.

The sun shall go out one day,
Like a big light bulb in the sky.
Do we live in darkness then,
No that's where new inventions become alive.

Ben Cook (13)
The Sweyne Park School, Rayleigh

Future Christmas

I wonder what will happen
In fifty something years
To Christmas as we know it -
And will we still be here?

Will lights be almost living -
And video games be real?
We might be a part of them
With sight, sound and feel.

Or maybe Christmas will be banned
By people shouting, *'Racist!'*
I really, really hope not -
As it will be sorely missed.

Jasmin Wetton (13)
The Sweyne Park School, Rayleigh

Party!

Meet up with your mates
For a birthday treat,
Why not go bowling?
Bowling, bowling, bowling,
Ball running down the lane at the speed of light,
Crashing into the bowling pins, aiming for a strike.
Bowling, bowling, bowling, what can I say?
Having fun is my favourite game,
My friends scream, 'Hooray!'
I'm slightly disappointed,
This time I have only got a spare,
My mate was unlucky,
Not getting any pins,
But we are having fun,
And that is what matters to me!
How about a meal after bowling
To quench your thirst
And keep hunger at bay?
Why not go to TGI Fridays?
Having a lovely meal with your friends.
After the meal,
Everyone can see my mates all singing to me!
Why not have a slumber party?
Maybe a pillow fight
Or tell secrets that have never been told before.
Everyone in the room vows not to tell a soul of what has been said.
You can do dares,
And if you are still not tired, carry on till morning light.
If you are, lay your sleepy head down onto your fluffy pillow,
And say, 'Goodnight!'

Nichola Todd (13)
The Sweyne Park School, Rayleigh

Stream Of Consciousness About The Future

New technology
Helping us cure diseases
Better governments
World peace
Aliens living on Earth
Hardly anything to eat
We only eat a pill a day
It keeps us healthy and fit
No more exercise
Flying cars
Don't cause pollution
Living on Mars
Earth explode
Earth uninhabitable
War
Atomic holocaust
Everyone dead
Alien invasion
No religion
Proof of no God
Sun exploded.

Marc Wesley (13)
The Sweyne Park School, Rayleigh

The Future!

The future's colours are golden sandy yellows.
The future will taste like the sea, sand and paella.
In the future you will smell the sea, chlorine and a whiff of fish.
In the future you will see a very peaceful, calm and fun place to be.
The future will sound like the wave splashing up against the rocks,
The sun blazing, children laughing and adults gossiping.
The future will feel clear, fresh, relaxed but energetic and clean.
To sum it all up the future and will be exciting for you and me.

Nicole Evans (11)
The Sweyne Park School, Rayleigh

England

England lost one-nil against Ireland
It was a disappointing game,
Which caused the supporters shame
But the Irish did play dirty in the game!

David Beckham put the free kick just right of the bar,
The ball just curved an inch too far.
Shaun Wright-Phillips, what a star,
He smacked the ball which hit the crossbar.

The ball dropped into the keeper's hands,
The Irish strikers had plans to score,
Which they did
And their fans gave a mighty roar.

England gave up, there was no hope.

The ref ended the game with a blast of his whistle.
England need to win the next two matches,
I hope that they try
Or we can kiss the World Cup goodbye.

Alex Blackmon (14)
The Sweyne Park School, Rayleigh

The Future's Orange

'The future's bright, the
future's Orange'
And the phone networks
are just that.
The noises are of
phones ringing
and it smells of radiation.

Bradley Race (11)
The Sweyne Park School, Rayleigh

The Future

You will never know what the future will hold
So lively and full yet so big and bold
Our future generations
Have all the complications
So many lives to live
So much help to give

With robot teachers
And abstract features
The future will bring
Cars that sing
Many houses with robot kids
Dustbins empty with padlocked lids

All these crazy things
Is what the future brings

So come on Future we are ready now
Give it your all and make us bow.

Laura Walker (14)
The Sweyne Park School, Rayleigh

My Future

Basketball all-star is what I wanna be,
Shooting and dunking for my country,
If I practise hard and grow seven-foot three,
2012 Olympics is where I'll be.

If I'm good enough,
I'll go to the USA,
Play college basketball,
And maybe NBA.

I'll be the next Michael Jordan,
And be a millionaire,
Win slam dunk competitions,
And I'll be jumping in the air.

Matthew Sharp (13)
The Sweyne Park School, Rayleigh

The Metal Future

I step into my metal house,
Through my metal door.
I'm walking in my metal shoes,
Along my metal floor.
I'm talking on my metal phone,
To my metal friends.
I'm walking to my metal school,
Down a path that never ends.
I'm sitting in my metal chair,
In my metal class.
I'm listening to my metal teacher,
Who's strangely made of brass.
I'm walking down the metal hall
And up some metal stairs,
Keep walking past some metal rooms,
Full of metal chairs.
I get some metal homework,
Go back to my metal home.
Cos in this shiny, metal world,
You're totally on your own.

Alex Furber (12)
The Sweyne Park School, Rayleigh